W9-DHU-736

DISCARD

DATE DUE

Demco, Inc. 38-293

Developing
QUALITY CARE
for
Young
Children

Developing
QUALITY CARE
for
Young
Children

HOW TO TURN EARLY CARE SETTINGS INTO MAGICAL PLACES

Nettie Becker ✦ Paul Becker
Foreword by Rebecca Shahmoon Shanok

CORWIN
PRESS
A SAGE Company

For information:

Corwin Press
A SAGE Company
2455 Teller Road
Thousand Oaks, California 91320
www.corwinpress.com

SAGE Ltd.
1 Oliver's Yard
55 City Road
London, EC1Y 1SP
United Kingdom

SAGE India Pvt. Ltd.
B 1/I 1 Mohan Cooperative
    Industrial Area
Mathura Road, New Delhi 110 044
India

SAGE Asia-Pacific Pte. Ltd.
33 Pekin Street #02-01
Far East Square
Singapore 048763

Printed in the United States of America

Library of Congress Cataloging-in-Publication Data

Becker, Nettie.
  Developing quality care for young children : how to turn early care settings into magical places / by Nettie Becker, Paul Becker.
      p. cm.
  Includes bibliographical references and index.
  ISBN 978-1-4129-6565-1 (cloth) — ISBN 978-1-4129-6566-8 (pbk.)
 1. Day care centers—Psychological aspects. 2. Child development. 3. Early childhood education. 4. Early childhood education—Parent participation. 5. Parent and infant. 6. Parent and child. I. Becker, Paul. II. Title.

  HQ778.5.B43 2009
  362.71'2068—dc22

2008017817

This book is printed on acid-free paper.

08   09   10   11   10   9   8   7   6   5   4   3   2   1

Acquisitions Editor:	Jessica Allan
Editorial Assistant:	Joanna Coelho
Production Editor:	Appingo Publishing Services
Cover Designer:	Michael Dubowe

Contents

Foreword

To Learn the ABCs, Children First Need to Master the Six Cs:
Interpersonal Experience Sets the Template for Life

Kindergarten teachers have estimated that 35 percent of America's children start school unprepared to learn (Boyer, 1991). In 1998 teachers in another national survey reported that about half of all children have problems making the transition to kindergarten (National Center for Early Childhood Development and Learning, 1998). When we fail to make the most of this important period in young children's lives, we set the stage for later difficulties; for example, many of these children will have difficulty learning to read.[1]

It has become a fact of modern, industrialized life that many young children spend the majority of their waking hours being taken care of in groups outside their homes by someone who is not their parent. More than thirteen million babies, toddlers, and preschoolers—approximately six out of ten children under the age of 6 who are not enrolled in kindergarten[2]—receive regular care from adults other than their parents.

Even while substitute care of very young children in classroomlike groupings has dramatically increased, it has become evident beyond doubt that the first five years of life are terrifically important: they set patterns that continue to have an impact for the rest of life.[3] What do children need to know to be ready for kindergarten and elementary school? What life experience supports robust development? Massive amounts of scientific evidence accumulating at an accelerating pace over the last six decades indicates that the quality of relationships— the abilities of parent or other caregiver and child to enjoy and expand their connections over months and years—has a deep impact on the ways in which little children grow across most domains of development. These domains can be summarized as the six "*Cs*," which are necessary for good citizenship and success in life: concentration, cognition, communication, curiosity, cooperation, and conscience. With brain development itself now shown and known to be dependent upon interpersonal experience across domains, a good relational start from the beginning sets the foundation for success in school and in life.

Dr. James Heckman, the scholar who won the Nobel Prize in economic sciences in 2000, demonstrated that investment in the very young makes not only good human and family sense but also excellent economic sense. He wrote:

> Learning starts in infancy, long before formal education begins, and continues throughout life. Research in psychology and cognition demonstrates how vitally important the early preschool years are for skill formation. Significantly, this is a time when human ability and motivation are shaped by families and noninstitutional environments. Early learning begets later learning and early success breeds later success, just as early failure breeds later failure. Success or failure at this stage lays the foundation for success or failure in school, which in turn leads to success or failure in post-school learning. Therefore, formal or institutional education is only one aspect of the learning process, albeit an important one, and research indicates that it is not necessarily the most important one. . . . The later in life we attempt to repair early deficits, the costlier the remediation becomes.[4]

In the United States

- One in five children has a diagnosable mental disorder.[5]
- Factors that predict mental health problems can be identified in the early years.[6]
- Children and youth from low-income households are at increased risk for mental health problems.[7]
- The younger the child, the greater the risk of poverty. Some 42 percent of children under age 6 live in low-income families.[8]
- Preschool children face expulsion rates three times higher than children in kindergarten through twelfth grade—a factor partly attributed to lack of attention to social-emotional needs.[9]

One might imagine, based on these facts, that federal, state, and local governments would rush forward to spearhead investment in our nation's young children by providing—and offering incentives to the private sector to provide—optimal child care. Yet the pathetic reality is that child care in this country for very young children remains woefully deficient.

"Both parents and child care teachers bear the burden of the current inadequate funding system. Clearly, parent fees put high-quality early care and education out of reach for many working families. Yet, this system also perpetuates low salaries, which fail to attract and retain highly skilled teachers. The impact is negative for all involved—child care providers, families, and children—and ultimately, for our nation as well. Low-quality early care and education put children's development at risk, including the development of abilities associated with reading success."[10]

Child care quality is usually measured by studies that fall into two categories: structural and process. "Both [categories] examine factors that support the responsive and reliable relationships with caregivers so essential for health development" in young children. Structural measures such as child-staff ratio and group size are approaches to research about child care whereas, in contrast, process measures shine a light on children's experience with their caregivers: their warmth, their attention, and their responsiveness."[11]

According to a videotape produced by WestEd, five million infants and toddlers are currently in child care in the United States. Furthermore, researchers indicate that 91 percent of group care serving infants and toddlers is inadequate and does not meet their basic needs, and that 40 percent are unsafe and harmful to development.[12] What could become a remarkable opportunity to support young children's development is being squandered. Just at the most impressionable time of their lives, a period characterized by vulnerability and promise, inadequate child care becomes yet another risk factor for the young and, especially, for the economically disadvantaged children of our nation.

The presence of one risk factor, such as poverty, together with any others—such as trauma, parental substance abuse, poor child care or school, and single-parent household—cumulatively increases the likelihood of later problems.[13] In New York City, 63,000 children—more than 50 percent of all our babies—are born into poverty, which is a major risk factor for early school failure and other difficulties later.[14] But, "where, after all, do universal human rights begin? In small places, close to home—so close and so small that they cannot be seen on any maps of the world. . . . Such are the places where every man, woman, and child seeks equal justice, equal opportunity, equal dignity."[15]

It is with these pressing realities in mind that *Developing Quality Care for Young Children: How to Turn Early Care Settings Into Magical Places* by Nettie Becker and Paul Becker has been written. The book's power is in its details, which utilize nuances from the "small places"; here a child care center. With detail of everyday moments in everyday lives, they breathe life into principles gathered from the study of many fields over decades. And, in fact, the younger and more vulnerable children are, the more they can benefit from guidance gleaned from *across* disciplines.[16] In the vitality of little interactions improvised between people that the book describes, big things are happening. Between small children and the grown-ups at the Rosa Lee Young school, learning and growing are unfolding, hand within hand, and often with a smile. This child care center is an inspiration, and *Developing Quality Care for Young Children* is, itself, a dedicated little miracle that wisely selects the principles it cherishes as chapter headings:

- The Little House on Village Avenue: What Makes a Good Child Care Center
- The First Task of Early Child Care: Building a Trusting Relationship Between Caregiver, Child, and Family

- The Second Task: Developing Wholesome Peer Relationships Among Children
- The Role of Curriculum and Staff Development in Early Child Care
- The School as a Reflection of Our Diverse Heritage
- High-Quality Child Care as a Learning Experience

If the six Cs form the basis for success in school, *Developing Quality Care for Young Children* provides the map on how to get there in group care and the belief that children can truly achieve those foundational capacities in groups that have nurturing teachers, respectful and committed to each child and parent.

This little book brings to mind what Adlai E. Stevenson said in 1962 about Eleanor Roosevelt: "She would rather light a candle than curse the darkness, and her glow has warmed the world." The Beckers provide the light of substance for child care workers, directors, teachers, graduate and undergraduate educators, policymakers, and "their" children alike, and its messages are a lamp into the darkness: clear, warm, and true.

Rebecca Shahmoon Shanok, PhD, LCSW
Director, Institute for Infants, Children and Families,
Jewish Board of Family and Children's Services

About the Authors

Nettie Becker has devoted her entire professional life to working with young people, first as a teacher and counselor of high school students, and for the past twenty years in the field of infant and early child care. She holds a master's degree in professional studies, majoring in dance/movement therapy that combined movement and psychology in the development of young children. She is a full member of the Academy of Dance Therapists Registered. She is also trained in the Kestenberg movement profile analysis that evaluates movement patterns and personality.

She has designed, set up, and implemented a movement program of adaptive physical education at a school for special children and has worked as a child development consultant for day care programs in New York City. She has also taught parenting classes in the continuing education department at Molloy College in New York.

She currently conducts parenting workshops in child development and movement through play for parents and their children in community library programs in Nassau County, New York. These workshops are designed to help parents engage with their young children through motor, sensory, and emotional stimulation that support their healthy mental and physical development. She has also introduced a community program for the parents of infants to help them engage with their babies through motor, sensory, and emotional stimulation in their first year of life.

Becker is a fellow emeritus in early childhood group therapy at the Child Development Center of the Jewish Board of Family and Children's Services and was part of the program's continuing education committee that served as a consulting group for child care professionals.

She is coauthor of *A Comprehensive Guide for Caregivers in Day Care Settings*, published in 1999. That book arose out of her observations and experience in a number of early child care settings that were not beneficial, and indeed often harmful, to children. Some of them are discussed further in the course of this book. She currently serves on the board of trustees of the Rosa Lee Young Childhood Center in Rockville Centre, New York, where, by contrast, she has been gratified to observe a high-quality child care program and its positive effect upon the children it serves. This book is the result of her observations of the school and its children, teachers, and staff.

Paul Becker, a high school teacher for many years, is now a writer and editor. He is the author of many articles and has edited a number of publications in the field of education and public policy. Along with Nettie Becker, he is coauthor of *A Comprehensive Guide for Caregivers in Day Care Settings*. For several years he was the editor of *Between the Lines*, a newsletter for writers in New York, and currently is the editor of a monthly newsletter on American industry for an economic research firm in New York.

Authors' Note

By all accounts they were very ordinary people. None had ever made the history books, and most are now forgotten. Surrounding them was a community that looked at them sometimes strangely, sometimes with hostility, but never as equals. They were the first generation not born into slavery and they had made their way to this little spot on New York's Long Island in search of work and a piece of life. They settled on the west end of Rockville Centre because it was a fairly well-off community and there was work, as domestics and handymen, in the homes of the white families around town.

She was one of them. An ordinary woman. The youngest of seventeen children born to a former slave. Up from Virginia a few years after dawn was breaking on the twentieth century, she eventually made her way to New York City to live with a sister, until she took a train one day to Rockville Centre to work as a nanny in the home of a wealthy banking family that lived in the town.

Over the years she and the others did not have to go south to be reminded of the precariousness of their existence. In a neighboring town, Freeport, where many of them went to worship at the A.M.E. Bethel Church, the Ku Klux Klan was growing. In 1924, when its influence peaked, some 30,000 townspeople looked on approvingly as the Klan marched 2,000 local members through Freeport's streets led by the town's chief of police.

In these early years of the new century, the small black community built its life—it worked and struggled, married and raised children. And she along with them. She met Charles Young at the A.M.E. Bethel Church. He was eighteen years her senior and had a responsible job as an armed courier delivering money by trolley to Wall Street banks. They married, bought a house in the village's west end (the first African American family to own a house in Rockville Centre), and had four children. A woman who strongly encouraged education, she taught her children, and later her grandchildren, to read before they started school because, she said, "What you learn in your head cannot be taken from you."

The flu epidemic of 1918 wreaked havoc on the family. Her husband died and her oldest child and only son, Charles, was rendered blind and deaf from the fever. After her husband's death, she took in laundry and worked as a domestic in village homes, determined to keep her house and hold her family together.

A very ordinary woman. But ordinary people can often become extraordinary. In 1941 as the nation was on the threshold of entering the Second World War, there was a school in the village called the Clinton Avenue School. It had eighty-two students, seventy of them black and twelve white. Once a school with a regular curriculum like all the other schools, it was now a place where white students were assigned because they were judged by the board of education to have "disabilities." A school with twelve white children "with disabilities" and all the black children in the town. The black children were taught in classrooms that combined different grade levels. They were taught how to "serve" whites. The boys were trained in how to be janitors; the girls in how to clean and cook and sew and iron. The board of education came there for lunch, often marveling at how well-trained the children were. Their teachers would send them out to do food shopping for the board lunches, and they made sure the board members were served in a clean and comfortable setting.

There was only one hitch. The children, some as old as 12 and 13, could print only block letters. They couldn't read well or write or spell. They were being sent to school to learn, but they were not learning anything that would enrich their lives.

And the very ordinary woman became part of the movement that organized a march on the school, back in 1941, long before the civil rights movement changed the face of the nation. Her youngest daughter, Ethel, led the battle, and the woman and another daughter, Hazel, devoted themselves to persuading parents to keep their children home to let school officials know that they wanted them to have a real education. The Rockville Centre Board of Education must have developed dyspepsia over its lunch to see these people, ordinary people, standing up and fighting to change their children's preordained station in life. And their efforts eventually led to the building of a new school in Rockville Centre, a regular elementary school attended by black and white children, with and without disabilities, learning together.

Some years later she went to work as a teacher's aide in a nearby town in a school for children with cerebral palsy. She spent the last years of her working life with these children, her dedication enhanced by her experience with a child of special needs of her own.

The woman died in 1972 at the age of 86. Her death came just weeks before a child care center in Rockville Centre named in her honor and dedicated to serving all preschool children of working parents, black and white, affluent and poor, opened its doors. And although the woman never made it into the history books, she has lived on for more than thirty years in the faces of the children who have passed through its doors.

This very ordinary woman was Rosa Lee Young. This book is dedicated to her memory.

Notes

The names of all the children cited in this book have been changed to protect their identities.

Excerpts from *Developmentally Appropriate Practices in Early Childhood Programs Serving Children from Birth Through Age 8* have been reprinted by permission of the National Association for the Education of Young Children.

Letter to the editor from parents Kenneth and Michele Fishgrund has been reprinted by permission of the *Rockville Centre Herald*.

All photos are courtesy of Rosa Lee Young Childhood Center.

Acknowledgments

I am indebted to many people in the writing of this book. There are those directly associated with the school itself and those who helped to prepare me to appreciate a school like Rosa Lee Young, the work that it does for young children, and the importance of such an institution in our society.

First, I am profoundly grateful to those at the school:

The administrators and the staff for their cooperation in opening their doors to me.

The school's director, Jeannine Rey, for the time she spent with me and for allowing me free access to the classes and teachers.

The teachers who welcomed me as an observer into their classrooms and spoke to me about the work they do each day.

The Rosa Lee Young board of directors and its chair, Catherine Pucciarelli, who devote so much of their time to the school out of their love and commitment to it.

The parents who spoke with me about the role the school has played in the lives of their families.

Without the cooperation and the blessing of all of these people from its very inception, this book would not have been possible.

I am also deeply grateful to two of the pioneers who started the school, Gloria Wallick and Director Emeritus Joan Sheppard. Their work and accomplishments are described in the prologue to the book. Here, just let me convey my appreciation for the time they gave me in interviews and in sharing with me some of the joys and heartbreaks over the thirty-five year history of the school.

There are also those organizations that have prepared me to be able to evaluate and appreciate the work that a school like this does for children.

A number of professional organizations stand out. In the early childhood field, we cannot underestimate the nationwide role played by Zero to Three National Center and the National Association for the Education of Young Children, whose conferences, books, publications, seminars, and campaigns on behalf of young children in America have been instrumental in promoting the welfare of these children as one of our national concerns. On local levels so too have the Boston Institute for the Development of Infants and Parents and the New York Zero to Three Network. All of them have been key players in my professional growth. And not the least, the American Dance Therapy Association, through its resources and professional conferences, has been an important source of my training in understanding and working with young children and their parents.

The two-year fellowship I spent with the Early Childhood Group Therapy program of the Jewish Board of Family and Children's Services, whose high-quality services and programs play an essential role in the lives of so many parents and children, prepared me, probably more than anything else, for the task of looking into and appreciating the work child care centers like the Rosa Lee Young school are doing.

I have also been very fortunate in being able to work with Jessica Allan, a highly skilled editor at Corwin Press. The comments and suggestions she made have immeasurably improved the quality of this book.

Most of all, I am indebted to the children at the Rosa Lee Young school. Many things make a high-quality child care center what it is, but in the final analysis, it is children like these all over our country who make it all worthwhile.

Additionally, Corwin Press would like to gratefully acknowledge the following peer reviewers for their editorial insight and guidance:

Denise Humphries
Preschool Principal
John F. Kennedy American School of Queretaro
Queretaro, Mexico

Rob Mocarsky
Kindergarten Teacher
Forest Hills School
Jackman, Maine

Diane Salverson
Inclusion Specialist
Early Childhood Direction Center
Buffalo, New York

Kerry Williams
Learning Community Facilitator
Wayne State College
Wayne, Nebraska

Prologue to a Dream That Came to Be

The history of a child care center is not often thought of as something worthy of mentioning, even in a book about child care. There is no mystery or intrigue and rarely any charismatic figures with well-known names. We recount in very brief summary here some of the highlights in the story of the founding of the Rosa Lee Young Childhood Center only because we wish to show how a few people with a vision and an understanding of the needs of their community can rise above the obstacles and prejudices of their time to create something beautiful: an institution that has meant so much in the lives of thousands of children in the community over the years. And we tell it because we know that the experiences we talk about have probably been duplicated by others in the field who also believe in the mission of high-quality early child care and who are making it a reality in towns and cities across America.

They certainly never thought of themselves as pioneers, these eight women. Nor, in their minds, were they doing something out of the ordinary. They were middle-class women, most with college backgrounds, some who were working and some staying home to raise families. But all of them were aware of a growing need in their community. And they decided to do something about it.

More and more women in and around their village of Rockville Centre were working outside the home at regular jobs, some part time, some nine to five. And many of them still had preschool age children, which meant that they couldn't rely on the kids' being supervised or cared for during the day. Some of the women were leaving the children with grandparents; others were left in the care of women who used their homes to take in some children of working parents during the day. If the working women could afford it, they hired nannies. It was a hit-or-miss proposition. Sometimes you got good child care, sometimes you didn't. For people with lower incomes, there was the federal Head

Start program, begun during the Johnson administration, to give children over the age of 3 a boost before they started school. It was a preschool program that was meant to compensate children from poorer families for any gaps in their preschool years that a child from a more advantaged background may have had. In addition to school readiness, it also provided nutritious breakfasts and lunches, and attended to some of the children's health care needs. Over the years it has earned high praise from educators for what it has been able to accomplish. Many children from low-income families were cared for during the day by Head Start and received their first learning experiences in the program.

But what if the family income was initially higher than the Head Start guidelines? Or what if the child was in Head Start and the mother's income now raised the family earnings above the Head Start level? A woman in this situation was plain out of luck. She either opted for some hit-or-miss child care, or she was forced to stop working to care for her child until he reached school age. A terrible dilemma faced by so many women, particularly if that woman had to work to help sustain the family. Eight women in the community looked at the situation—and they acted.

Among the eight were several with a keen interest in early childhood education and development. Several were active in the National Council of Jewish Women, others in the League of Women Voters. Two of them were destined to play key roles. One was Gloria Wallick. Married shortly after she graduated from Brown University, she had forsaken a career for a number of years to raise a family in the Rockville Centre home she bought with her husband back in the sixties.

In 1972 a book called *Windows on Day Care* appeared, authored by former director of the Women's Bureau of the U.S. Department of Labor, Mary Dublin Keyserling. It was a report on the coming critical need for early child care based on the findings of the National Council of Jewish Women (NCJW) and published by that organization. Much of the information in the book came from NCJW sections around the country. The book, Wallick recalled, was "a very powerful impetus" in beginning to call attention to the rising problem. Although there were far fewer women in the workforce than there are today, "as people bought homes and moved out to the suburbs, there were certain costs that were involved" and more women began to work to add to the family income. Although organized programs of child care go back to the settlement houses in the late nineteenth century, this was the first time that the child care problem was reaching national proportions.

In the 1970s, as the youngest of her children neared graduation from elementary school, Wallick began to pick up her interrupted career, earning a master's degree in public policy and management and working as director of the Day Care Council of Nassau.

Joan Sheppard, the second of the two women who played the key roles, had taught in elementary school for three years before she left teaching to raise her family. In 1972 she completed her master's degree in early childhood education and began looking for a job in the public schools. But she had the bad luck to hit the teaching job market at just the wrong time. In the early seventies, budgets were being cut. In New York City even some tenured teachers were being laid off. She was pondering her next steps when Gloria Wallick, the chair of the advisory committee for Rockville Centre's Head Start program, asked her to join the committee. It was in this capacity that the two began to wrestle with the problem of working mothers whose children could not get into Head Start, either because there were no longer any openings or because they had "incomed out" of Head Start, even if they still could not afford child care otherwise.

The basic educational underpinning of Head Start was one that both Wallick and Sheppard embraced: its commitment to the idea, in Sheppard's words, that "early child care was not just day care." It's not babysitting. It is engaged in establishing "the foundation for learning." In a high-quality child care program, children are exposed to interesting, exciting things and need to be able to question and explore. The feeling among all the founders, in Sheppard's words, was, "There was so much more we could be doing for children, that it wasn't enough just to provide a lot of toys—in our case, although we started out with a lot of begged and borrowed toys, eventually we were able to get all the good toys we needed—but that wasn't enough. We had to hire people and implement a program that really respected children. That was the main thing children need. When you have a child in your care for that many hours a day, you can't just be a teacher. You've got to be a nurturer, a confidant. You've got to be a good parent."

Sheppard credits Wallick with coming up with the idea of starting a new school dedicated to bringing top-quality child care to working parents regardless of income. They gathered the group of eight women together and decided that they first had to establish the community's need for such a center. The eight then became the steering committee of the larger group of volunteers they activated, mainly from the National Council of Jewish Women, which had taken on the issue of child care nationwide, and the League of Women Voters, which had always been active on community issues. The dining room table in Wallick's home became their first "office." The school district, which conducted a regular survey on children of preschool age to plan for future enrollments, granted them access to these records. They then sent a letter to the families of the preschool children and followed up with door-to-door interviews conducted by eighty women from the two organizations who had volunteered their time. Their aim was to find out if there was really a need and *if the need crossed class and income lines*. This was the second vital element of the program they envisaged. Because Head Start was limited to families on the lowest rungs of the economic ladder, it inevitably tended to become a segregated program. Wallick and Sheppard had lengthy talks about it, about the need for such a program for children from *all* the rungs on that ladder. They saw clearly that a large portion of American children, not just poor children, needed early child care.

As Wallick emphasized, "I always felt very strongly and so did Joan and the other people who subsequently worked with us, that a good early child care program should be open to everybody." Of course, this creates another problem. It means that you have to have money to provide scholarships for people who cannot pay for the full cost of care.

The response from the community was a surprise even to those conducting the survey. Rockville Centre was typically an upper middle-class community, at least the majority of its residents were, not the kind of town in which families are generally thought of as needing two incomes to make it. Not the kind of town in which parents are generally thought of as badly needing child care. Of the 170 questionnaires sent out, about 100 were returned, most of them responding favorably to the idea of setting up such a program. The response was a microcosm of what was happening in the country but not getting the kind of wide attention it deserved.

Public agencies like the local economic opportunities councils were approached to see if the new school could get some scholarship money on a sliding scale based upon family income for those who could not afford the full tuition, even as every effort was made to recruit children from varied income strata.

The survey, follow up, and compilation took several months to complete. Once the need was established, the next hurdle arose. From the beginning the center faced "three main obstacles," in the words of Joan Sheppard, "money, money, and money." Like so many community projects today, the money question has been a struggle throughout the thirty-five years of the school's existence. Just to start, organizers needed seed money to rent a place that satisfied the licensing requirements for a children's center, including space, fire safety, and sanitary rules. They had to furnish it; hire the first staff members, which meant setting aside money for a payroll; buy toys and educational equipment; make sure they had insurance coverage; comply with state child care regulations; and take care of all legal matters and a whole set of other things that go into the opening of any enterprise. And then there was the need to establish tuition rates at a reasonable level for parents and, at the same time, enable the school to cover its costs. And they had to find a way to get some aid for scholarship money for those parents who could not afford to pay full tuition. All this took time, complicated by the fact that the people involved were all volunteers who were doing this in their spare time.

A local government agency promised some seed money to begin the project. But, when it came time, the agency reneged on the seed money it promised. "When we lost that, a lot of people were discouraged," Sheppard recalled. "But Gloria never lost faith." She struggled. She cut corners. She was a ubiquitous presence in the offices of government and community agencies, cajoling, pushing, and pleading. Acquiring a little something here, a little something there, just so there was enough to get it off the ground. She was finally able to secure a contract with the Department of Social Services to provide scholarship money for those children whose families were income eligible for scholarships.

Somewhere along the line, the question of a name for the center came up. A dear friend of Joan Sheppard, who had been active in civil rights in Rockville Centre, knew Rosa Lee Young and her family very well, and knew of the role she played in the community (see Authors' Note). She suggested the name to Joan, who relayed it to the board, and the board liked it.

Meanwhile, with barely a shoestring but plenty of audacity, the women pushed forward. The eight-member steering committee was reconstituted as the Board of Directors. In turn it appointed one of the eight women on the steering committee, a former administrator in the Head Start program, as the school's first director. The board rented two rooms in the basement of a local church, one of whose founders had been Rosa Lee Young, and went about furnishing them and working to comply with all the state requirements for operating a child care center. Toys were bought, borrowed, and contributed. Joan Sheppard's 9-year-old son, her youngest, combed through boxes of his old toys, long stored away, and donated his prized set of blocks "for the children."

And thus, in August 1972, the Rosa Lee Young Childhood Center—only a dream of eight women a few years earlier, women who worked and begged and pushed, who bounced off walls of resistance and bureaucracy and rose to push again—opened its doors and became a reality. But while it may have been a triumphal moment, the problems, as they say, were only beginning.

The question of money continued to plague the new enterprise. The school started with no money and a debt for the rental of the rooms. It meant that, initially, there was no money for payroll. But in an extraordinary act of dedication to the new project, the small staff worked without pay until money could be obtained to meet the payroll. For six weeks they worked for nothing. Then, as word began to get around, more people inquired about enrolling their children, and some tuition money started to come in. Staff members still couldn't be paid their full salaries; only slowly was the school able to increase payments until staff members could take home the full compensation due them. Some staff members were supported by spouses for the time they were unpaid and could get by for a while. Others, not in this position, struggled but held on. The enthusiasm of the school's director, who worked tirelessly in those first days to get the school moving, was an important stimulus to the rest of the staff. In any case, without their sacrifice the school could never have gotten off the ground. As Sheppard reflected upon it, she couldn't help being struck by a mixture of pride and vexation. Pride in the dedication of that staff and vexation that, in a sense, this is the ever present problem in the profession. "People who worked in child care were seen as giving everything and getting very little," she said. "That is something I've spent a good deal of my time in later years trying to overcome so that we could pay people a decent wage."

In the weeks and months after the program began, the register of children expanded. Volunteers wrote notices for the local community newspaper. Another mailing went out to parents who had responded positively to the original questionnaire letting them know the project was indeed up and running.

But the money problem has continued to plague the school right up to the present day. Sometimes the Department of Social Services was late in paying its bills. Other times there was difficulty with parents being authorized as qualifying for scholarship subsidies because case workers would run the parents through hoops, causing many of them to become discouraged and withdraw from the program. And because the children whose families were being assisted with scholarships constituted about a third of the enrollment, it was money that the school desperately needed to function.

One source of funds has been extremely helpful over the years. For a long time now, the center has benefitted from a yearly grant through the efforts of the local New York State senator who lives in Rockville Centre. The senator, Dean Skelos, was for many years the assistant to the majority leader of the State Senate. He recently became the majority leader. He has provided Rosa Lee Young with $15,000 each year out of the state discretionary funds at his disposal for worthwhile community projects. Also from time to time, Rosa Lee Young has been the recipient of small grants from some local foundations.

As more children were enrolled, the space at the church, not the best to start with, became increasingly inadequate for their needs. The board looked around for larger facilities. Two years after its founding, the school moved to larger accomodations in another church, where it remained for the next seven years. During those years the school continued to grow, as did the overall need for early child care facilities in the community. Over the first eight or ten years, space concerns dictated that the school consist of only preschool children, ages 3 through 5. But by the early eighties, the need for a toddler program for children as young as 18 months became apparent as more mothers were compelled to leave their children at an earlier age to seek employment.

This need prompted the board to come to a decision. They had to have their own building with enough space to accommodate the need. The problems that a racially and ethnically integrated school—even one that served only very young children—ran into in trying to purchase a property in what was virtually an all-white community were formidable. Many of us have become familiar with some of the uglier aspects of this issue, but a description of its workings here would take us into another area that is beyond the scope of this book. Finally, a real estate agent showed them the house on Village Avenue. The woman who owned it was the widow of a dentist. It had been a professional office as well as a residence.

"I can remember vividly when we went to the contract signing," said Sheppard. "Marie Rothschild was the president of the board. The school had all of $12,000 in the bank. We were committing ourselves to paying Mrs. Quint, the woman who sold it to us, $50,000 at the closing with a balance of $43,000 to be carried in a mortgage. The woman looked at Marie and said 'I hope you're going to be able to do this.' And Marie, summoning all the *chutzpah* at her disposal, looked right back at her and said, 'Would I be signing my name if I couldn't do this?' as she signed and wondered if the world was going to come down on her."

But then the board mounted a campaign to raise the money. Several husbands of board members persuaded their companies to donate, and the mayor of Rockville Centre at the time, Leonard Sandel, also came through with some money. When the time came for the closing, the board had the $50,000, and Rothschild was spared the world's coming down on her.

From its conception up to the present day, the school could never have survived without the help of many volunteers—people of good will in the community who donated their money and their services to the school. There were legal matters that have been handled *pro bono* by a very fine lawyer. When the school finally acquired its own place, there was the massive job of renovation to convert a dentist's office and residence into classrooms. It was done by a local resident in the construction business who volunteered his company to be the general contractor, *gratis*, leaving Rosa Lee Young with having to meet only the cost of labor and materials. A talented architect also donated his services *pro bono*, devoting much time to drawing up the plans for renovation and defending them before the State Department of Social Services.

The school finally moved into its new house in 1981 with four classes: one class of 10 children who had recently turned 3 years old, two older prekindergarten classes of twelve and fourteen children each, and a kindergarten class of sixteen children. In later years further renovations were made that turned the garage and back hall into classrooms, enabling the school to create another prekindergarten class and a toddler class. The prekindergartners were then organized into mixed 3- and 4-year-olds, allowing them to remain in the same group with the same teacher for a longer period of time, thus making for fewer transitions in their young lives. The center was actually now licensed for eighty-five children aged 18 months to 12 years. For the first time since the center started nine years earlier, the board and staff were actually in control of their school. After nine years, Sheppard said, "This is our home. This belongs to us."

Sheppard, in the meantime, had been honing her skills as an early childhood educator. With her master's degree in early childhood education in hand, she spent six years teaching classes in the center and supplementing her teaching experiences by attending conferences of organizations like the National Association for the Education of Young Children. She was already recognized by the board as a person who had developed into an outstanding educator and administrator when, in 1978, she was named the new director of Rosa Lee Young, a post she held for some twenty-five years.

Widowed for a number of years and now retired, Sheppard looks back on those years of struggle to establish and maintain this center and reflects. For people on both ends of the economic spectrum, affluent and not, this school, she says with pride, "has been a tremendous asset. Their children were in a place where they were not only cared for and safe, but they were in a stimulating environment which encouraged them to think and to create. There is no doubt we've had an impact."

She frequently looks at the graduating classes and the honor rolls of the middle school and high school in town to see how many of them got their start at the little house on Village Avenue. One recent year she saw a young lady on the eleventh grade honor roll at the high school who was at Rosa Lee Young as a preschooler and kindergartner. She was the child of a single mother who struggled all the way to give her daughter the best. The girl was an outstanding student, and according to the local paper, involved in the school dramatic production and a number of other school activities and was making plans for college. "She's a lovely young lady, and I think we were definitely a part of it." Sheppard recounts that she had met the girl's mother in the supermarket. The mother was "bubbling over at her daughter's achievements. She raised the child by herself. She needed a support system and we were there."

For more than thirty years, Rosa Lee Young has "been there" for people like this. And she is just one. Multiply that by hundreds or thousands of others over the years and you get the real impact this school has had. *And multiply that by the growing number of other centers like Rosa Lee Young around the country and the people who have made them possible and you get the full impact of what high-quality child care can do for us as a society.*

It's hard to say if Joan Sheppard or Gloria Wallick, now also widowed and retired, or any of the group of eight women foresaw the results of the toil they put into starting this project over three decades ago. All the ups and downs, the elation, and the disappointment. What is certain for anyone who looks at it, is that these were people who have left us all a legacy. In the spirit of Rosa Lee Young herself, these ordinary people, these people who don't make the evening news or get the limelight, have created and sustained something very noble. They are people of whom their community and their country can be very proud. They are real heroes in our time.

Introduction

The building is part stone and part frame. It stands on a quiet corner in a quiet town in New York's Long Island, and were it not for the playground equipment in the yard outside, it would be hard to distinguish it from the one-family residences that are its neighbors. It once served as the home and office of a dentist named Dr. Quint. For the past twenty-five years or so, in rooms where teeth were once drilled and filled and pulled, children from ages 18 months through 5 years now sit at little tables and draw or sit in the laps of their teachers to hear stories of bears and frogs or watch fascinated as butterflies hatch from cocoons.

For twenty-five years at the building and about ten years before that, the Rosa Lee Young Childhood Center has cared for the children of working parents who must leave their children in the trust of others each day while they pursue a livelihood. It is one of the early child care centers that seems to work, a place where parents can leave their children with confidence that they will be looked after and cared for and, yes, loved, for the eight or ten hours a day, five days a week, fifty-two weeks a year that they will be there.

It is a setting that inspires both hope and tragedy at the same time. Hope because within its walls you can see the tremendous potential of what an early child care program can do for children, tragedy because despite the vast need, places like this that provide quality child care for children are all too rare in our country today.

THE CRITICAL NEED FOR QUALITY EARLY CHILD CARE

Anyone who doubts the urgent necessity for high-quality early child care need only look at the profound changes that have taken place in American family life over the past forty years. These changes are reflected in the high rate of divorce and family breakups, and the big increase in families headed by a single parent. But the biggest change in family life has come through the large number of women now in the workforce, prompted by the fact that, in most two-parent families in our country today, at least two wage earners, both mother and father, are essential for the family's livelihood. This is a relatively new phenomenon in America where, until recently, the mother traditionally stayed home and cared for the children, and the father was the breadwinner. In the past, if a woman worked, she did so to enhance the family's income and move it to a higher standard of living. Today most women, including the mothers of very young children, work because they have to; because their incomes added to that of their husbands are critical in keeping their families afloat.

Just a quick examination of a few figures should make the point all too clear. According to census figures, in 2002, 10.2 million, or 60.8 percent, of all American mothers with children under the age of 6 were in the labor force.[17] The question that then starkly presents itself is: What happens to these young children with no parent at home to care for them? In many cases grandmothers are called upon to take care of the children. Such care might be good or not so good, but today with the need so vast, even this is obviously not a reliable factor.

Which brings us to the real problem we face as a society. We are not the only advanced industrial society with large numbers of mothers in the workforce; some others have a higher percentage of working women than we have. But the United States is one of the few industrial countries with no national system of early child care. And this problem is escalating rapidly. In 1991 the Washington, D.C.-based National Association for the Education of Young Children reported on a national child care survey: "23% of babies younger than 1 year of age (many younger than six months and some as young as five and six weeks), 33% of 1-year-olds, 38% of two-year-olds, and 50% of three-year-olds are cared for outside their homes in regulated and unregulated family child care and in infant/toddler centers."[18] By 1999 the percentages of young children being cared for by those other than a parent had risen to 44 percent for infants under one year, 53 percent of 1-year-olds, 57 percent of 2-year-olds, and 61 percent under the age of 4.[19] The 2002 census reported that 56.8 percent of mothers with children 1 year old or younger, 62.1 percent with 2-year-olds, and 65 percent with children between the ages of 3 and 5 were now in the labor force.[20] "Early and extensive enrollment in child care has become the norm in U.S. society," notes *From Neurons to Neighborhoods,* the landmark study of early child development in the United States by the National Research Council and the Institute of Medicine. "Indeed, if children were only sporadically or briefly exposed to child care, it would not be the visible policy issue that it is today."[21] Or, in absolute numbers, "Of the 21 million children under the age of six in the United States, almost 13 million are spending at least part of their day in child care. For the first time, large numbers of children are being cared for by those with no emotional investment in them."[22]

But faced with this compelling national need for early child care, the response on the part of national and state authorities has been incredibly inadequate. Many child care facilities charge tuition fees well out of the range of ordinary working families. One on Long Island, not far from Rosa Lee Young, charges from $975 to $1,260 a month, depending on the age of the child.[23] Others exist on an almost hand-to-mouth basis, often scrounging to come up with ideas to raise funds to continue operation. Rosa Lee Young is a private, non-profit school. It receives some money from federal, state, and county governments administered through Nassau County's Department of Health and Human Services (formerly the Department of Social Services). Like many other facilities of this type, Rosa Lee Young must engage in numerous fundraising activities to cover its operational expenses and to provide scholarships for those who cannot afford the tuition. The scholarships are important in maintaining the institution as one that serves parents from across economic lines.

Another factor that weighs heavily on the profession is staffing. In a field that should insist upon people with the highest educational and professional skills, the pay is shockingly low; in many cases hardly above the poverty line, with people often leaving the profession to seek other jobs where they can make a living. At a national conference in 1996, sponsored by Zero to Three, a professional organization dedicated to the healthy development of infants and toddlers, J. Ronald Lally, EdD, director of the Center for Child and Family Studies in Sausalito, California, highlighted the problem in chilling terms. He flatly declared at that time that only 10 percent of the day care centers in the United States can be considered good and that 40 percent actually did harm to the children. At the same time, another study reported that only 14 percent of child care for all age groups was considered adequate, with the percentage of adequate care even lower for infants and toddlers.[24]

For years early childhood educators seemed to be talking in the wind. As the number of women in the workforce with young children at home grew, pioneering organizations like Zero to Three and the National Association for the Education of Young Children wrote and campaigned, sponsored professional conferences and workshops, and tirelessly sought to upgrade the profession and focus the attention of the nation on the growing need for quality, affordable early child care. And for years, as the problem of the shortage of such child care facilities multiplied, very few seemed to listen.

Until recently.

In recent years the press has been reporting that more people are beginning to pay attention to the acute need for early child care. An article in *The New York Times* highlighted the problem and the growth of a new "child care industry" in the suburban communities of Long Island, New York, where Rosa Lee Young is. According to the *Times*, a study commissioned in 2004 by the Child Care Councils of Nassau and Suffolk counties, groups that collect data and provide parents with information about child care facilities, found that about 74,000 children on Long Island were cared for out of the home during the day. About 85 percent of them were in day care centers and nursery schools, with the rest cared for in the homes of individual caretakers. Many day care facilities on Long Island, said the study, were booked to capacity and had waiting lists. They generated revenues of $612 million a year. "With that kind of money on the table," said the *Times*, "child care is attracting entrepreneurs as well as nurturers, who are carving out market niches and offering a wide variety of services and settings." Child care centers that have long provided high-quality professional care are understandably worried, not about the competition but about the fact that in the absence of strict national and state standards, the quality of care can suffer.[25] The *Times* article also pointed to the concern among child care professionals that the "entrepreneurship" factor is leading many to forsake long-established principles of early child development in favor of catering to the current popular notion of preparing children for tests, even at the earliest ages.

And, of course, for a problem like this one, which has not been addressed for so long, it is going to take a lot more pressure to bring it up to the priority status it deserves in America today. As recently as October 18, 2007, a piece in *The New York Times* by its op-ed columnist Gail Collins was notable for the fact that very little had changed in the way of national attitudes toward early child care over the past two decades. Criticizing the 2008 presidential contenders competing in the primaries of both political parties for completely ignoring the problem that has become so vital for millions of American families, she declared, "We live in a country where quality child care is *controversial* [italics in original]. . . . Right now, the only parents who routinely get serious child care assistance from the government are extremely poor mothers in welfare-to-work programs. Even for them, the waiting lists tend to be ridiculously long. In many states, once a woman actually gets a job, she loses the day care. Middle-class families get zip, even though a decent private child care program costs $12,000 a year in some parts of the country." For a single parent with two children in child care, that's larger in some states than the parent's entire median income. "For child care workers," Collins noted, "the average wage is $8.78 an hour. It's one of the worst-paying career tracks in the country. A preschool teacher with a postgraduate degree and years of experience can make $30,000 a year." And although certification is needed for many jobs less critical in national importance than this, only twelve states require any training to take care of children, Collins reported.

New York State, to be sure, has certain basic rules for its licensed centers, such as the number of children a center can admit based upon the age of the children, the space available, and the number of staff members. It also stipulates that anyone caring in a home for three or more children not related to the owner must be registered with the state, and anyone with access to the home over 16 years of age must be fingerprinted. The facility must also be certified as safe and sanitary by local officials.

Nevertheless, as people in the field maintain and as we repeatedly illustrate in the pages to follow, although these factors are basic, there is much more to quality child care than this. I have had some of my own troubling encounters with child care centers over the years in which I have observed practices that were harmful, often even abusive, to young children. And that's what makes the story of the Rosa Lee Young Childhood Center, and others like it, so significant. And so inspiring.

In this book we'll examine some of the basic principles of high-quality early child care and how it can be applied in everyday practice in one current child care center. The first chapter discusses the general philosophy and qualities of what makes a good child care center, why Rosa Lee Young seems to be working so well, and how this all begins with the youngest children. In subsequent chapters we dig more deeply into specific aspects of the program at Rosa Lee Young—how it establishes an environment that fosters healthy and creative relationships among the children and between children and adults; how it uses this creative environment to build communication skills among children and prepare them for school; how it acknowledges and uses the ethnic and cultural diversity of the children in its care to prepare them for participation in a nation and a world that is also diverse; and how it strives to maintain the professional standards of its administration and staff in the face of some of the difficulties we've noted above.

Of course, we never intend to imply throughout this book that Rosa Lee Young is the only high-quality child care center in the nation. We have written about this particular school because it is the one we have become familiar with. But, throughout this great country there are people, dedicated people, who are striving to make a difference in the lives of children. They struggle every day with the same problems Rosa Lee Young has and despite it, they provide children with the early experiences that can make a big difference in their lives. For those who work with children, it is a very exciting and heartwarming story.

The Little House on Village Avenue

What Makes a Good Child Care Center

Ye (children) are better than all the ballads
That ever were sung or said,
For ye are living poems
And all the rest are dead

—Henry Wadsworth Longfellow

This is such a happy, encouraging, magical place.

—Linda Schnitzer, a teacher at
Rosa Lee Young Childhood Center

In the introduction to this book, we discussed the critical need for a system of affordable child care throughout our country. But there is more to early child care than merely caring for children while parents work. This chapter discusses the basic qualities of a good child care center. Specifically, from practical classroom illustrations in the toddler classroom, it shows

- How a skilled practitioner works with children as young as 18 months to convey the love and warmth they need while beginning the process of education
- How the teacher stimulates toddlers' imaginations and encourages them to communicate their thoughts and feelings
- The physical facilities in a quality child care program that encourage developmental play in children and allow them maximum opportunities to explore as individuals and in groups
- The family support services that such a program should offer

It also discusses the difficulties in maintaining a high-quality professional staff in this field and how a quality program can help to reduce high staff turnover.

The village of Rockville Centre is just a thirty-five-minute ride on the commuter train from the heart of Manhattan. Its neat, one-family homes on tree-lined streets reflect a generally middle-class character, along with the many professionals and business people who commute daily to work from the village.

The Rosa Lee Young Childhood Center is near the center of town, on the quiet corner of North Village and Wilson avenues, just across the street from a building housing professional offices and a block or two down from the town's fairly substantial library. Its irregular shaped yard on one side, which measures about 40-by-15 feet, holds the usual brightly colored slides and climbing apparatus for young children. On the other side of the house, a smaller yard also serves as a play area.

Walk through the front door into its small entrance hallway and you are in narrow off-white painted corridors, cheered by the brightly colored posters and the pictures of children and staff members that adorn its walls. On the ground floor, is the tiny, cramped administrative office, home to the center's director, social worker, and two other administrative workers.

About 10 feet from the main office, the corridor splits into a T-shape, with a classroom on either side. The walls outside each room are lined with hooks for children's coats. The classrooms themselves on the ground level are large; one is the former garage of the house, which now is the room for the prekindergartners. Each classroom is divided into different areas by standing bookshelves and cubbies housing toys. In addition to a central, or common, area where children gather for meals or circle time, there is an art area, an area for blocks and construction toys, a family area with dollhouses and dress-up clothes for children and dolls, and a reading area. Just off the entrance, the house's former living room nurtures the toddler group, the youngest group in the center. A stairway outside the administration office in the main corridor leads upstairs to two more classrooms.

The school could use more space. Lack of space has prevented it from instituting a program for infant care. As we noted in the introduction, a majority of mothers with children *under a year old* are now working. But the youngest group at Rosa Lee Young is the toddler class; the youngest child at the school is 18 months.

"We would like to have an infant program, but we don't have the space here," said Jeannine Rey, regretfully.

Jeannine is the school's recently appointed director, who has been working at the school for more than thirty years.

"Many working parents of the toddlers and prekindergartners have infants that they have to leave somewhere else. It would be so much more desirable for them to be able to have their children in the same school, not only for the convenience but also from the children's perspective. It's so much more like a family when the older children also have their baby siblings here."

QUALITY CARE IS NOT JUST DAY CARE: HOW A GOOD EARLY CHILD CARE PROGRAM PREPARES CHILDREN FOR LIFE

Although the physical plant of a school is important, as most educators will tell you, what makes or breaks any child care program is the staff—teachers, aides, social workers, support staff, administrators—who perform the daily tasks of

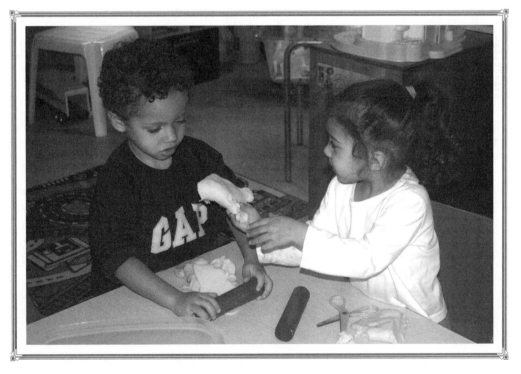

Playdough sculpture is fascinating.

caring for the children. And that care must entail the daily application of a program based upon the best scientific knowledge of the needs of children and how they grow and develop physically, emotionally, socially, and cognitively.

"What do we mean by child care?" asked the authors of *From Neurons to Neighborhoods*. "It is not just *day care*. It is also not just *care*" [all emphasis in original]. Citing previous studies, they affirm: "Beneficial outcomes for children in early child care are associated with settings that provide both nurturance and support for early learning and language development . . . and preparation for school." This is a far cry from the kind of day care in which large numbers of working American women are forced to leave their children with a babysitter or nanny, many of whom only minimally interact with children, often keeping them occupied by sitting them in front of a TV screen for a good part of the day. "Child care," emphasized one noted authority, "must be understood as a profound influence on the life of children, not as a service to parents like A.T.M. machines."[26]

Over the years, a number of philosophies have addressed the most beneficial ways to work with young children. One that has had a great deal of influence on Rosa Lee Young is the *Reggio Emilia approach* (see Appendix C, pages 151–154). However, not all the principles of this approach can be duplicated in other places, and Rosa Lee Young, although influenced by the Reggio Emilia method, has adapted it and made use of other educational philosophies as well. Most schools of thought, far from contradicting each other, overlap, stressing settings that provide the maximum opportunities for nurturing and creativity, and allowing children to explore the world around them. In general, they borrow heavily from the works of Lev Vygotsky, who stressed the connections between play and cognitive development in children, and from Jean Piaget, who believed that "a child's intelligence unfolds through her own interaction with the environment"[27] rather than through formal instruction. These schools of thought stress the developmental approach to early child care, with some advocating more open classrooms and less teacher instruction than others do. The Montessori school in early childhood education, for example, strives to place children in one or two, three-hour uninterrupted work periods each day that are not broken up by larger group activities. Montessori also stresses constant peer interaction, child-to-child teaching, and socialization.[28]

Other advocates of the developmental approach to early child care, such as Zero to Three and the National Association for the Education of Young Children (NAEYC), stress developmentally appropriate programs for children at different stages and the quality of relationships between peers and between adults and children in the program. "Child care," they maintain, "depends on caregivers who are knowledgeable and skilled, and committed to creating and sustaining these relationships."[29] Their approach is not the totally open classroom cited earlier, but one with somewhat more structure. The clearest presentation of their philosophy is the National Association for the Education of Young Children's "Developmentally Appropriate Practice in Early Childhood Programs" in Appendix B.

Throughout this book, we also draw from the work of prominent child care authorities such as Stanley I. Greenspan, T. Berry Brazelton, Lesley Koplow, and

Alicia Lieberman, who write about early child care as a combination of emotional, social, psychological, and cognitive development.

Rosa Lee Young and many other child care programs like it are heavily influenced by developmental philosophies of Reggio Emilia, NAEYC, and others that stress practices that are developmentally appropriate while not completely unstructured. It is important to emphasize in this connection that children cannot be straitjacketed. Not all children benefit from any one child care program; some benefit from one type of child care, some from another.

At the same time, good child care must not be confused with formal schooling. That's an important point these days. In the recent rush to prepare children academically for school, a major factor has been left out of some child care programs: Reading to them, telling them stories, and asking them questions and then encouraging them to tell you their stories, or playing alphabet games, will prepare them for reading far better than will the drills on letters of the alphabet and phonics.[30] (For a fuller discussion of this question, see Chapter 6.)

For the infant, the toddler, or the preschooler, no learning can take place without love and the warmth of a relationship between the child and the teacher, who is really the child's substitute parent for most of the day. Summing it up, Zero to Three wrote: "Perhaps most important, we have learned to appreciate the role of relationships in every aspect of early development. Infants and toddlers develop expectations about people's behavior and about themselves based on how parents and others treat them. Through daily interactions with responsive affectionate adults, babies experience their first positive love relationships. Trust and emotional security develop when infants learn that their needs will be met predictably and consistently. Self-confidence develops as babies and toddlers learn to communicate their needs and master challenges in their world."[31]

When we use the term *child care*, declared the authors of *From Neurons to Neighborhoods* emphatically, we mean "the blend of care, nurturance, and early education that the best child care provides."[32] And that's how this book uses the term *child care*, which is the only meaningful way that the real needs of young children are met.

"When it comes to child care, there are many aspects to quality, but I really believe that quality comes from those people that are administering the program and working in the program, your professional staff," emphasized Rosa Lee Young Director Jeannine Rey. "The leadership of the staff must be professionals who understand developmentally appropriate theory and practices. You have to have a leader who's really embedded in early childhood education and a staff that is professional and educated and can understand and implement a developmentally appropriate philosophy and curriculum. In the end, you can have the best material, you can have all the money in the world, but if you don't have a staff that's educated and professional, you're not going to have a quality program."

How this plays out at a high-quality child care center like Rosa Lee Young is the subject of this book.

THE TODDLER CLASSROOM: WHERE A SKILLED CHILD CARE PROFESSIONAL CAN OPEN UP THE WORLD TO CHILDREN

No one ever calls her Paula, the name with which she was born. For the fifteen years she has been at Rosa Lee Young, the staff, the parents, and the children have known her only as Pepper Robinson, the loved and respected teacher whose classroom to many children has been the first step on the road to their education.

A woman with expressive blue eyes that smile easily, she glides around her classroom, moving from one child to another with an easy, flowing rhythm. Everything she does in her class with the children and her coteacher, Jennifer Gordon-Fray, is done with the gentle confidence of a professional who knows exactly what she is doing and is always in charge. Most significantly, there is no question that she enjoys her work with children.

Pepper is the teacher of the toddler group, eight children ages 18 months to 3 years. *In her classroom every day, she provides the practical application of the philosophy developed by modern child care theoreticians over decades of work and research.* And although she is obviously a person of great energy, her pace in the classroom is deliberately slow and controlled.

"Many of these children's lives are hectic," she explained, "with parents working and a full-day schedule from early morning until evening. They need a calming atmosphere in their daily activities."

When I visited her class in early May, a particularly cold winter that had lasted longer than usual was just receding into spring. April had been unusually cold, and the bloom that usually comes in that month was late by several weeks. Trees were just beginning to bud, and spring was fighting to finally come out and be recognized. At eight o'clock in the morning, parents on their way to work arrived one at a time to drop off their children. All the children except for the toddlers are dropped off in one room where there are special toys and materials for the children to play with before the day's routine actually begins. The toddlers and the 2- and 3-year-olds go directly to their room. It is a familiar place to them, their home for the rest of the day. And, as on all other days, Pepper was there waiting for them as the first two parents arrived with their children, two robust little boys who moved with ease into a familiar classroom. There was Carlos, a 22-month-old Hispanic child with a round face, dark hair, and large black eyes, and Kirk, an African American child of 2-and-a-half years, quick witted with an already large vocabulary for his age. Pepper exchanged warm greetings with the parents and the children, and asked the parents how things were going. They spoke for a minute or two as the children hung their coats on their assigned hooks. The parents left, and within a few minutes, the boys were sitting in her lap near the window. Led by Pepper, whose questions prompted them to observe and describe, they talked about the trees outside and how it was raining.

They sat there and talked for about ten minutes until other children began arriving. One was Robin, a 2-and-a-half year old white child, brought in by her mother. After the teacher and parent again exchanged warm greetings, Robin's mother spoke about a christening she and Robin attended over the weekend. Part of the familiarity that children feel toward their child care classroom is accomplished by establishing an atmosphere that is, in many ways, an extension of the children's homes, with children constantly observing their parents in familiar and cordial relations with their teachers.

Robin is a very active child physically. She moves quickly and has a tendency to dominate the others. She brought a doll with her from home, and Pepper reminded her that she had to put her doll away for now. (Toys brought from home are a necessary comforting factor to a child, but they tend to become a distraction that prevents the child from participating in the group activities.) Robin approached me and gave me the doll to hold for a few minutes before taking it back and placing it on a nearby table. Pepper then put the doll on a shelf, a safe place for it but out of view for the rest of the day. It was a way to avoid problems later on.

At the side of the toddler room is a "water table," a rectangular table with a set-in plastic tub that the teacher fills and the children use. They fill small plastic cups, pails, and other containers and empty them, a repeated process that children at this stage love. During the first 3 years of life, they learn mainly through sensory motor stimulation, perceiving things around them and moving in reaction to them. Water is a soothing substance that can keep children at this age busy for long periods observing and figuring out how it pours, how it looks, and how it feels.

As Carlos poured out a container into the tub, he said, *"Agua."* Pepper repeated the word. *"Agua, sí."* She said to him, "Water. *Agua.* Water." At 22 months, Carlos may already be in the first stages, aided by his child care experience, of becoming bilingual.

When the children looked as though they were ready for another activity, the teacher, whose experience had tuned her in to such moments before they became problems, said with animated enthusiasm, "Let's take out the horses." The children agreed. The three horses were brought out from the toy area and the children all rocked on them.

At one point, Robin started to push Carlos off a rocking horse, and Pepper had to gently remind her, "We don't touch his body," a euphemism for "no hitting or pushing." Robin, without protest, went to another horse.

After a few minutes, Pepper walked over to the section where books stood on a shelf and her voice took on a tone of excitement.

"Let's read a book! Which book shall we read?" She pretty well knew the answer.

"The Three Bears," chorused the children. No surprise to Pepper because the book was on the table in front of her, and various objects representing the characters in *The Three Bears* were ready in a box to be used. Although her manner with the children made it look like a spontaneous occurrence, it was obviously well planned. She told me later that this was their favorite book.

They gathered around almost as if on signal. They had done this many times before. They knew what book time and story time meant.

Pepper read the story to them. Her face was animated and alive as her voice changed to represent the different characters in the story. Watching her, I couldn't help being reminded of the words of one of my professors of education back in my college days years earlier. "There are people who are scholars, devoting their lives to acquiring knowledge and dispensing it to others. There are those who are psychologists, getting inside the heads of people to discover what motivates them and gets them to act. There are those who are social workers, taking care of people's problems and needs. And there are actors, artists who know how to connect with their audiences to put across ideas and emotions. Well, a good teacher has to be all of these things."

When the story was over, the children asked Pepper to read it again, which she did. Then when she finished, she went to the box that seemed to be sitting there just waiting to be used. She took out a bunch of drawn and constructed flannel figures, each one representing a character or an object in the story. There was the Mama Bear, the Papa Bear, the Baby Bear, Goldilocks, the house, the cereal bowls ("Someone has been eating my porridge"—remember?), the beds ("Someone has been sleeping in my bed"), and so on. She also had a board to which the flannel figures stuck. She asked, "Where is Goldilocks?" and children pointed her out. She asked one of them to pick up Goldilocks and bring it to her, and she placed it on the board. She did the same with all the other characters and objects, singing about the story in the different voices of the characters as she placed them on the board. I thought for a moment that things would get a bit troublesome when Robin took one of the bowls from Carlos, but Pepper calmly said to Robin, "Carlos is going to work with you on the bowls. Who needs Papa Bear's bowl?" Robin said she did and Carlos handed it to her while he picked up another bowl. After all the objects were placed on the board, Pepper told Kirk to take them down and put them away so they could go on to another activity. But Robin took one of the bowls back. She wanted it. Kirk looked perplexed because he was supposed to put them all away. Pepper told him reassuringly that Robin would give it to him when all the rest were put away. Such moral persuasion Robin found hard to resist. She surrendered her bowl and then said, "Goodbye, I'll go play horsey."

All the classrooms at Rosa Lee Young have a main section where children participate in group activities and class projects, and smaller sections around the room to which children go to play alone or in small groups. Essential to this approach is a classroom that allows children the fullest freedom of expression, a balance of space that takes into account the physical, psychological, and cognitive needs of the children. Classrooms are divided into many different areas: a central area where children can gather with their teachers in one class activity and individual areas around the room where children can engage in their own creative pursuits. These areas can differ from school to school and class to class. There should be an art area where children can express themselves with crayons, colored markers, paints and brushes, paper, glue, scissors, yarns, ribbons, and anything else that supports their ability to express their thoughts and emotions creatively. Other areas could be, but are not limited to, a dress-up area where children can act out their ideas through dramatic play; a reading area where children can take books off shelves and look through them or where a teacher can read to a child individually or in a small subgroup; a computer area where children can engage in games and gain computer skills; a construction area where children can work on building projects with blocks, Legos ®, and other construction toys; and so on. (For a more comprehensive view on the implementation of this setup, see Chapter 4 on the Rosa Lee Young curriculum.)

It was to one of these areas Robin went now to be by herself, diverting her aggression by rocking vigorously on a horse.

Pepper recaptured the situation to me later. "You have to always understand: these are toddlers. They're not developmentally there yet. You can't be generous unless you're full. You can't understand the concept of sharing unless you have grown and developed into someone who feels satisfied with himself. Some are beginning to acquire it; some take a little longer. That's why patience is an absolute necessity at these tricky moments."

TRANSLATING PRINCIPLES INTO PRACTICE IN A GOOD CHILD CARE PROGRAM

To a casual observer, Pepper's handling of the children here was nothing extraordinary, just a natural sequence of events in the classroom. That's what really makes it so exceptional. Like a natural athlete who makes a great play look easy, Pepper's actions in her class follow the theories and philosophies developed by modern child care advocates and practitioners, and she puts them into natural use in virtually every operation of her classroom.

Daily Separation: The Preschool Classroom as an Extension of Home

From the moment Pepper greeted the first children and their parents, it was obvious that both parents and children were very much at ease in her classroom. These, after all, are only toddlers who would have problems separating from parents if they were not completely at home. But they immediately went to their coat hooks to hang their coats and did not hesitate to sit on her lap and talk about trees a few minutes later. It was an established routine they knew well, and, judging from the ease of the children, it was not something that was imposed by fear but by a mutual love and respect. The parents, too, obviously felt welcome right from the beginning as they all exchanged greetings and spoke for a few minutes. When the children said goodbye to their parents, it was an easy parting. The children knew a familiar day was coming and were not frightened by it. "The key to quality care is the quality of relationships— relationships between the infant and her family, between child and caregiver, between caregiver and family, and among adults in the child care setting," wrote one prominent authority.[33]

Elaborating on this theme, Alicia Lieberman wrote: "Child care is first and foremost about relationships. It is about how to separate from the parents with trust that they will come back. It is also about forming new relationships with the caregiver and with other children that will be enriching and sustaining in the course of the day." Infants and toddlers, she continues, can be expected "to do well when they can learn over time that separations are predictable and lead equally predictably to reunions, that caregivers are emotionally available, and that parents and caregivers are accepting of the child's ambivalence about separations."[34]

When the toddlers at Rosa Lee Young separate easily from their parents each morning, it is because their experience tells them that their caregiver, very much like their parent, is there for them and will satisfy their needs and that the center is another home to them. This isn't the kind of atmosphere that comes overnight or by accident. It is built up through much work and skill over the course of the school year by a practitioner who knows how to do it and whose heart really believes in it.

The Emotional Connection Between Caregiver and Child

When the children sat in Pepper's lap and they talked about the trees and the rain outside, they were learning about the world the only way a toddler can learn, through an emotional connection with the caregiver, whether that care-

Measuring flour—skilled bakers at work.

giver is a parent or a teacher. "No colorful pop-up toy or computerized light-and-sound gadget can come close to matching the companionable lessons in problem solving that you offer your child as you play and engage in gestural dialogues together," said the renowned child psychiatrist Stanley I. Greenspan. "At each succeeding stage of development, we have found that emotional interactions like a baby's smile leading to a hug enable the child to understand how the world works, and eventually to think, solve problems, and master academic challenges. Emotions are actually the internal architects, conductors, or organizers of our minds. They tell us how and what to think, what to say and when to say it, and what to do. We 'know' things through our emotional interactions and then apply that knowledge to the cognitive world."[35] The process of establishing and maintaining this emotional link between caregiver and child is the subject of Chapter 2.

This pattern of learning and discipline through trust and love continued throughout the day. It was the essential glue that held Pepper's class together. When she reminded Robin in a gentle but routine way about the doll the child had brought from home, there was no fuss. The child gave me the doll and then appeared quite satisfied when it was placed on a shelf, in a safe place. Responses like this one are not easily established with toddlers; it takes a lot of hard work, patience, and a thorough understanding of what their needs are.

Reading Children's Cues

In all of the other activities in that initial half hour that began the day and, indeed, throughout the day, the teacher was constantly tuned into cues that children are always giving. She could read the children. She knew when they were interested and when they were ready for another activity. And she knew when some were ready and some were not and how to distract those who were not. Just a bit later, when Jennifer, her coteacher came in, it was easier for Jennifer to take one or more of the children who did not want to participate in the activity of the others and supervise them at something else while Pepper conducted the activity with the rest of the class. In all cases, it was the cues detected by an experienced teacher that were important in telling her when to move from one project to another.

This is a fundamental principle in a child care classroom—being alert and responsive to children's cues. They must know when to follow the initiative of the child, and when to let the child follow his own lead, "when to guide, when to teach, and when to intervene. Responsive caregivers are alert to signs of stress in each child's behavior and respond with appropriate stress-reducing activities and techniques. The responsive caregiver continuously facilitates the development of self-esteem by respecting and accepting children, regardless of their behavior."[36]

Pepper and Jennifer were constantly tuned in to the children and alert to act before problems arose. They knew when toddlers with a very short span of attention needed to change an activity and when they did not, when to continue to play at the water table, when to take out the horses, and when to read their favorite book and play games about the book. They knew the children who played well together and subtly paired them off, always making it appear as the child's choice. We saw this very clearly later when the children moved about to different activities: "Would Steven and Carlos like to play at the water table?" To Kirk and Margaret: "Let's play three bears with the flannel board." To Robin: "Aren't the dolls (in the family corner section of the room) nice? Let's see what they're doing in their house." Jennifer also knew when Robin's attention was flagging and when to ask, "Do you want me to play with you?" She knew when to spend time one-on-one with Robin and when to switch to the two boys at the water table. Pepper and Jennifer knew these things because they were sensitive to the children's needs, a sensitivity they had acquired through their training and their love of the children in their care.

"The tools for encouragement or correction are the same: reading and responding to a child's cues," wrote Kyle D. Pruett, child and family psychiatrist and professor at the Yale Child Study Center. "These cues are all emotional—the flicker of interest in the shy child, the wrinkled forehead in the bored child, the delight in the child who's just mastered a new skill, and the pout of a child whose exploration is suddenly curtailed." This doesn't mean, Pruett hastened to add, that every whim of a child must be catered to. But it does mean that all children, even very young ones, have a broad range of interests and emotions that should be understood and worked with. "Your child's emotional cues at this age let you know what's happening, and they give you the keys to unlock the best possibilities."[37]

From the water table to the reading of *The Three Bears* to the flannel board, the teacher consistently took her cues and direction from her reading of the children. Her skill provided the perfect example of methodology for all teachers of very young children; the children gave her the direction, but it was she who was always in charge.

Encouraging Children to Communicate Thoughts

Jennifer Gordon-Fray, Pepper's coteacher, is young and relatively new to Rosa Lee Young, having started there only a few months before. She arrived at nine o'clock bringing breakfast to the three children already there. Two more, Steven, a boy of 22 months, and Margaret, a 3-year-old girl, came in during breakfast and joined the group at the table. (Three of the toddlers were absent that day.) The breakfast of cereal, milk, and fruit is eaten at a table in one section of the classroom. The children moved their own chairs to a round table where the food was set up, although the younger children in the group needed a bit of help with the chairs. The teachers eat breakfast with the children. When you really get down to it, Pepper and Jennifer, in effect, are coparents, rather than teachers, to the children in their care.

"We are a family here," Pepper said to me later. "These children spend more of their waking time with us than they do with their own families."

The atmosphere at the breakfast table was relaxed as the teachers talked to the children and encouraged them to talk about almost anything as they ate.

When the children spoke, Pepper and Jennifer asked them questions. Sometimes they answered, and sometimes they paused, either searching for an answer or groping for the right words to say it. Sometimes, when they couldn't find an answer, they just went on to another subject. No matter what they said, the teachers encouraged them to talk—and to think.

"At the end of the second year of life," said Greenspan, "as communication for communication's sake begins to overtake communication merely to meet a need, the child embarks on a course he will continue throughout life. His love for his caregivers and the pleasure they bring him leads him to enjoy communicating in its own right. . . . The caring adult encourages the child to translate his immediate, concrete aims into words and images. . . . A child's first ideas emerge as discrete islands of thought with little relation between them. . . . As caregivers respond to symbolic expressions in both pretend play and the interchanges of daily life, in the third and fourth years the child begins to form bridges among his ideas and between his own thoughts and those of others."[38] Greenspan's advice: "Try to set aside time each day for reality-based, logical conversations with your toddler. If his attention flags and his thoughts seem to drift, gently bring him back to the theme of your conversation while empathizing with his desire not to talk, or to talk about something else. . . . Help your child learn to think by holding long conversations with her in which you seek her opinions rather than simply trade pieces of information."[39]

The principle is basic: *Caregivers should understand the connections between interacting with children and developing language and literary skills.* If a caregiver consistently interacts with infants, toddlers, and young children, she is constantly building the child's vocabulary, giving the child words to express ideas and emotions. As the child grows, by listening and talking to her and using simple words and sentences, songs, rhymes, and games, the caregiver is getting the child to understand that words have meanings. By reading stories to her, the caregiver is getting the child to associate the words and ideas with the pictures on a page and the pictures with the printed words. This transition from verbal interaction to vocabulary building to expression of ideas and emotions through spoken words and then through printed words creates a learning environment that is essential to encouraging the child to enjoy books and want to read. Sharing stories and books should be a natural part of every day's activities in a child care center.

Ideally, developing language and literary skills should begin even earlier than the toddler stage, almost from the time the baby is born. "Talking early to your baby helps your baby to learn about language," stressed two leading child care authorities. "How you talk with your baby makes a difference in how well he uses language even years later! Scientists who study children tell us that most children who use language well and do well in school have mamas and daddies [and, by extension, child care teachers, —N.B.] who talked a lot to them when the children were babies.

"Your baby learns how to make the sounds of language by listening to the sounds you make. He also begins to learn the names of things, people, and actions. Babies learn what different words mean as they listen to their special adults talk about an experience. Your child learns how to put words together to make sentences by listening to you talk in sentences. If you do not talk much to your baby, he will not learn much language. You are the most important language *teacher* [emphasis in original] for your baby."[40]

It goes without saying that what applies to the parent here also applies to the child care teacher, who is, after all, the child's substitute parent for most of the day. It also goes without saying that the process begun in infancy must be carried over into toddlerhood and beyond, into the school years. If a parent has not done this with an infant, the child care teacher has an even greater obligation to use her interaction with the child to build language and literacy skills to compensate for what the child has missed earlier, a task that is more difficult but that can be accomplished.

In the toddler class at Rosa Lee Young, Pepper and Jennifer engaged the children in conversations throughout the day. They answered their questions in sentences and language the children could understand. When a child became involved in a particular activity with a teacher or another child, the teachers either reflected on what they were doing or asked questions about it. They gave the children opportunities to think and express ideas. They worked together with the children and encouraged the children to work with each other to solve the problem at hand. The environment stimulated the children to feel comfortable enough to explore and express themselves.

As they sat at the breakfast table, the process continued. The children's conversation at that table, if put on the stage, could have resembled a Harold Pinter play in which the characters often talk past each other on different levels. But among toddlers, it's a perfectly logical sequence of expression. The conversation at breakfast went like this:

Carlos (spotting the milk): *Leche.*

Jennifer: *Leche,* that's right. Milk. *Leche.* Milk. (At this point, Margaret arrives, dropped off by her father. She moves in with ease, joining the group at the breakfast table, and he leaves.)

Margaret: My daddy gave me donut and chocolate milk.

Pepper: Daddy took you out for breakfast? (Margaret nods.)

Carlos (points to the milk): *Leche.*

Jennifer: You want milk for your cereal? (Carlos nods.)

Kirk (counting out his Cheerios): One, two, three, four, five, six, seven.

Pepper: Can I have a turn? One, two, three, four, five, six. (Pepper turns to the others and invokes the experience of the story she had read and played out with them earlier.)

Pepper: Who is the Mama Bear eating porridge?

Several children: Me!

Pepper: Who is the Papa Bear?

Several children (including some who had volunteered themselves as the Mama Bear): Me!

Pepper: And who is the Baby Bear?

Several children again: Me!

Pepper: And who is Goldilocks?

Same children: Me!

Margaret: It's raining outside.

Pepper: It's raining, it's pouring, the old man is snoring.

Robin: Julia was christened yesterday. My aunt Joyce is Julia's mommy.

Pepper: Is Julia your new baby cousin? (Robin nods.)

Pepper (cuts some apples into small pieces and distributes them to the children): What shall we do today on this rainy day? Maybe we should take out dress-up clothes? Good idea or not a good idea?

Margaret: My mommy has a baby in her tummy.

Kirk: I have a baby in my tummy.

Pepper (to Kirk): You have a baby in your tummy?

Margaret: No, only my mommy has a baby in her tummy.

Robin (getting up): I have to go to the bathroom. (She leaves for the bathroom, which is just a few feet away. Each of the classrooms has its own children's bathroom complete with a small toilet low enough to be accessible to small children.) (At this point, Steven comes in with his mother. After saying goodbye to his mother, he sits down next to Margaret, who is 14 months older than he.)

Margaret: I don't like him. I want to go home to my mommy.

Pepper (to Margaret): Babies can sometimes be annoying. How will you deal with it?

Margaret: I will keep my baby in a crib.

Pepper: What are you going to do if she bothers you?

Margaret: She won't do it. (At this point, it is worth noting that Pepper could have also said gently to Margaret: "I don't think Steven feels good when you tell him you don't like him." This gentle reminder could get Margaret to think about the feelings of another child, helping to build in her the quality of empathy toward others. As Greenspan reminded us: "Empathy is the hallmark of a great kid, but it's one of the hardest traits for a child to acquire. Although all children are born with an innate need to relate to others, they need examples and encouragement to be able to feel themselves in another person's shoes. This is a complicated cognitive and emotional task that grows and develops over time, with your help."[41])

Kirk: I want to be a doctor.

Carlos: I want to be a doctor, too. (Steven sits closer to Margaret. She looks annoyed with him.)

Pepper (to Margaret): He doesn't know how you feel. You will just have to talk to him. (Then, looking around for a moment) I wonder what Robin is doing in the bathroom. (Jennifer, who has been helping the children put their food into bowls, gets up to check on Robin.)

Pepper: Let's sing some nursery rhymes. Kirk, what would you like to sing?

Kirk: "I've Been Working on the Railroad."

Pepper (with a big smile): I knew it. It's your favorite song, isn't it, Kirk? (Kirk nods.)

Pepper (proceeding to sing while strumming on an imaginary banjo. The children, having been encouraged and knowing the cues, imitate her gestures on the banjo, say some of the words, and come in with an appropriate "toot, toot" on signal):

I've been working on the railroad

All the livelong day.

I've been working on the railroad

Just to pass the time away.

Can't you hear the whistle blowing?

Children (on Pepper's hand and facial signal): Toot! Toot!

Pepper: *Early in the morn.*

Can't you hear the captain shouting

Dinah, won't you blow your horn.

Children (again, on signal): Toot! Toot! (Led by Pepper, they all applaud.)

Pepper: What is the captain shouting?

Children (responding together, as it is obviously a familiar question to them): Blow your horn!

Kirk: Let's sing it again.

Pepper: OK.

They went through the song again. As this scene unfolded, my thoughts couldn't help but go back to another experience I had at a child care center several years earlier. It was a center that was part of a program for homeless mothers and their young children, where I served for eighteen months as a part-time consultant and staff trainer. The children were taken care of at the child care center while their mothers sought and found employment until they were able to find a place to live for themselves and their children. The child care program, like the shelter program itself, was run by a well-known national charity.

Both that facility and Rosa Lee Young were early child care centers for children, but here all similarities ended. At the former, most of the staff knew very little about the psychology or the developmental needs of children, and some of them couldn't have cared less. The children there also ate breakfast, but what a different scene it was. There was no talking at the table, except to ask for some food. No social conversation. No teacher encouragement of interaction or of the children's relating to each other. Basically, the rule that was enforced was the old-fashioned puritanical one that the table was for eating, not talking or other frivolities. Sit down and eat. That was it. A joyless place, and that atmosphere carried over into the rest of the child care program there. I tried to do what I could to change the situation but ran into a barrier of entrenched bureaucratic stonewalling. "That's the way we do things here. We know how to take care of these children." What a difference, I thought, as I watched the children at the breakfast table now.

Here, aided by the teachers, the children were encouraged to engage in pleasant mealtime conversation, and each expressed something important to him or her. The teachers listened to them and sustained a conversation with them. Pepper asked questions relating to the three bears story she had just read to them. When Margaret said, "My mommy has a baby in her tummy," and Kirk responded that he, too, had a baby in his tummy, Pepper understood how difficult it is for a child at this age to understand what this means. She kept the conversation going with a question but without any hint of laughter or sarcasm or disbelief that would stifle the thoughts of the children.

Earlier, when Pepper read the story of Goldilocks and the three bears, she gave the characters meaning by modulating her voice to simulate them. She asked the children questions about the role of the characters in the story. She answered their questions. She elaborated on the objects and characters in the story by using a board on which she stuck replicas of them. The children had a chance to describe what the objects in the story represented and what role each character played. Each of these actions is a vital step in the development of the process of connecting language to thinking and later to literacy.

Each Child Is Different and
Provision Must Be Made for These Differences

After breakfast, the children, guided by the teachers, cleared the tables, emptied the remnants of their bowls in the garbage can and brought them to the sink in the bathroom to be picked up later by the kitchen staff and washed. The remainder of the day's activities began. Pepper and Jennifer directed the children from their knowledge of them and from their understanding of one of the most fundamental principles of education: Each child is different, and in every classroom, particularly in the early years, provision must be made for these individual differences.

This phrase has become a cliché in most education circles. Most of us know it. However, despite the repetition of the principle, a common failing of most class situations is to attempt to mold all the children into one common pattern or activity. This is particularly counterproductive with very young children who cannot yet understand the need or the mechanics of group activities and are consistently distracted by different things. A caregiver must "understand the temperaments, moods, and preferences of each child" and "adapt sleeping, eating, and play activities to meet individual needs."[42] Caregivers should continually assess the children in their care for individual special abilities and disabilities. *The curriculum in the child care center should provide for these differences by providing an environment for a variety of activities, materials, and schedules to accommodate the developing needs of each child.*

Pepper and Jennifer understood the temperaments of each of the children in their class. They knew that Kirk could handle conflict without becoming too upset and that Robin had a temper that could flare up easily and needed more nurturing and understanding. They respected Carlos's need to speak Spanish, a language in which he felt more secure because it was the language spoken in his home. They made him comfortable when they repeated the words in Spanish and then translated them into English so that the child felt at home in both languages in the classroom. They understood the necessity of dealing with situations that a particular child is not developmentally ready to handle. Robin, for example, was not yet ready to negotiate and solve a problem with Kirk over possession of one of the flannel-board bowls in the three bears story, and Pepper stepped in to solve the problem in a way that both children accepted. Such a positive solution is not always possible, as every parent and teacher knows, but with a staff member that is both well trained and caring, it is more likely to occur than with someone who isn't as well trained. Knowing that Kirk and Margaret interact well together, Pepper said to them, "Let's play three bears," and led them to the flannel board to play with the figures in the story. She then did the same with the two younger children, Carlos and Steven, directing them to the water table where she stayed with them. Jennifer went to a part of the room called the family corner with Robin, where she set up a dollhouse with people inside. Jennifer then rotated between working with the girl in the family corner and the two little boys at the water table. After a while, Jennifer noticed that Robin's attention was drawn to her playing with Margaret and Kirk and that she could no longer concentrate on the dollhouse. "Do you want me to play with you?" she asked the girl. Robin indicated that she did, so Jennifer went over and played again with Robin and the dollhouse.

The developmental level of each child is a factor that a skilled teacher must be very much aware of. As children grow older, they are capable of engaging in higher

Soap and water get things clean.

and higher forms of symbolic play, that is, using objects to *represent* other things. They may use a dollhouse to represent a real house; a doll or a teddy bear becomes a real person to whom they talk; toy dishes become real dishes in an imaginary kitchen as they pretend to eat, and so on. At a higher stage, they might take a cardboard box and pretend it's a real house, or a spoon could become a person. Symbolic play, particularly as it takes on higher forms, requires a more developed sense of imagination, and children in a classroom situation are not all at the same level of development. Therefore, it requires that the teacher understand this and know which children to subtly combine into subgroups because they play better together. In the toddler class, Carlos and Steven, the two youngest, were encouraged to play together at the water table where they filled and emptied vessels while others in the group with a more developed sense of symbolic play were guided to the flannel board or the doll house. And, of course, the situation was constantly changing as children wanted to move to other areas. The teachers were constantly alert to the differences among each of the children and worked with them at every level. During most of the day, it was not getting the child to fit into one common activity for all but finding activities in which children at different levels of interest and development were comfortable.

Understanding and planning for each child's individuality is a bedrock principle in any good child care program, and no one sums up its importance more than two of the most noted authorities in the child development field,

Brazelton and Greenspan. "The degree to which we can tailor experiences to each child's unique qualities increases the likelihood of that child's growing up physically, intellectually, and emotionally healthy and thus able to meet the expectations of family and society.[43]

Pepper generally directed the scene, placing the children for a game or activity, most of the time by moving them in a particular direction with a firm, soft voice and a gentle touch. Her hands seemed to be constantly moving children or objects. Touch is very important to toddlers, who need the warmth of human contact. Pepper often picked the younger children up to soothe them or place them appropriately. *And she talked to them, always talked. She talked about what the children were doing, what interested them, repeating the words that went with the actions many times.*

Encouraged to communicate, the children also spoke to each other. Kirk and Margaret talked to each other about the flannel figures they were placing on the board, reenacting the story of Goldilocks. Their conversation was limited by their young age, but they were beginning the art of communication, and their child care experience is helping to sharpen this skill that is so necessary for later success in school.

After a while, Kirk grew tired of the flannel board and went over to Robin in the family corner. "I want to play with you," he said. Visibly disappointed, Margaret called out to Kirk, "Play with me." She didn't want to be deserted. Alert to a sign of possible trouble, Jennifer went over to Margaret, pretended surprise, and exclaimed, "Oh, Goldilocks ran away. She must be hiding somewhere. Maybe the three bears want to go to sleep now." Obligingly, the toddler put the three bears to sleep and then joined Jennifer who subtly led her over to the family corner where all three children—Kirk, Robin, and Margaret—now played with the doll house.

And so the day went on. And as it did, it became more apparent that you could not observe the workings of those teachers and children without realizing that virtually all the elements of what the books say a good child care program should be were translated into concrete terms in that classroom. All the abstractions of the researchers and the child care experts suddenly came to life in the ordinary operation of a classroom in which professionals worked with young children every day, week after week, and month after month.

HIGH-QUALITY CHILD CARE: SOME OTHER BASICS

In this chapter, we have used the toddler class at Rosa Lee Young to touch upon some basic principles by which skilled teachers in a classroom work with very young children. We will use observations in other classes at the school in subsequent chapters to more deeply illustrate these and other principles and techniques in early child care.

But there is more to the story of a successful early child care center than this. To run a successful program and to maintain the kind of skilled teachers that are necessary in such a program, there are other important qualities that a

The Physical Setup of a Child Care Center

A number of studies, books, and articles on the physical needs of a child care center should always be kept in mind. They are outlined briefly here.

Provision for the health and safety of the children. This includes clean and well-planned areas for food preparation and toileting; nutritious breakfasts and lunches; indoor and outdoor equipment that encourage children to climb, crawl, run, and jump. It also includes careful planning to avoid hazards like sharp pointed furniture and electrical outlets.

A *carefully planned physical environment appropriate to the age level of the children.* This includes well-planned play space; soft lighting; plenty of storage space for a wide variety of toys—picture books, clay, blocks, wheel toys, and puzzles that challenge toddlers and preschoolers—of different sizes, shapes, and textures; crib mobiles and hard-paged books for infants; and convenient diapering areas. Also essential is a nearby refrigerator and storage space for the snacks and drinks that young children need frequently in small amounts during the day.

Small groups, particularly for infants and toddlers, with high ratios of staff to children. Child care professionals have recommended that no more than six children who are not yet mobile should be in a group, and one caretaker should be responsible for no more than three young infants. No more than nine children who are crawling or walking (up to 18 months) should be in a group, with a caretaker responsible for no more than three mobile infants. For children 18 months to 3 years, group size should be no more than twelve; staff-to-child ratio, 1:4.

Assignment of a primary caregiver to each child and continuity of care. It is generally recommended that from the time the child first enters child care, regardless of her age, one primary caregiver should be the professional principally responsible for the care of that child. It is also generally recommended that to the greatest extent possible, there should be continuity of care; that is, the primary caregiver should follow the child from her infancy until at least the age of three. In most American child care centers, the principle of continuity of care is very difficult, if not impossible, to follow because of the high turnover of staff personnel (see pages 23–27).

For a more in-depth discussion of physical criteria for an early child care center, see Lally et al., *Caring for Infants and Toddlers in Groups,* op. cit., pp. 29–43; Nettie Becker, op. cit., Chapter 2, pp. 22–29; Graham, et al., op. cit., pp. 14–16; Lella Gandini, "Fundamentals of the Reggio Emilia Approach to Early Childhood Education," *Young Children,* National Association for the Education of Young Children, Nov. 1993, p. 6.

school must have. They can be roughly divided into three categories: the physical setup of the center itself (see box above), the support services it offers to children and their families, and how a quality staff can be maintained in the face of serious obstacles in the profession.

The Support Services Offered to Children and Their Families

Rosa Lee Young has a full-time certified social worker, Barbara Andrzejewski, who has worked there for twenty years. She has a multitude of responsibilities, a couple of which are maintaining the record of each child's health history and keeping up-to-date links with community services on children's health and well-being. She also provides crisis counseling for parents and children when the need arises, as it did after the terrorist attack on the United States on September 11, 2001. Many children saw the scene, repeated over and over on TV, of the planes crashing into the twin towers and the buildings collapsing, and reacted with terrible fear that their world would also collapse. She consults, when necessary, with a nurse practitioner on questions affecting the children's health.

The Staff Is Aware and Makes Use of Comprehensive Community Support Services for Children and Families

No child care program can meet all the needs of a child's family. In many cases, a child or his family needs the help that only outside community agencies can give. It is, therefore, essential that a child care program maintain ongoing linkages with those community agencies to provide social services and medical, mental health, and therapeutic interventions when necessary.

Barbara Andrzejewski is responsible for maintaining such linkages. Among those are services provided by the Nassau County Department of Health, the county in which the school is located, and the local school district. They are available on request for private evaluation of the children recommended to them and for early intervention when necessary. The social worker also closely coordinates with a number of county and state agencies that provide specialists to work with children with special needs: special education counselors, speech therapists, physical therapists, and others. All these special services are provided only with the consent of the parent of the particular child. They are completely voluntary, but most parents will take advantage of them if they have confidence in the school that is arranging the services. *A very important feature of this service is that the professionals provided by the agencies will come into Rosa Lee Young so the parent does not have to travel to some remote location.*

It seems so self-evident that linkages to such services must be an absolutely necessary part of every good child care program; yet with such a wide disparity in the quality of child care and so many centers, operating with or without licenses, this vital part of a good child care program often does not exist.

The Family and Cultural Background of the Children Must Be Understood, Respected, and Carried Over as Much as Possible Into the Classroom

A good child care program reflects the cultures and values of the children's families in its curriculum. Efforts are made to link the child's home language and cultural norms into the class's daily routines, with the teacher exhibiting pride in the diverse cultures of the children in her care. The school "should communicate each day with families, welcome parents into their child's classroom, and organize special events that include the child's family members."[44] As mentioned earlier, the child should be able to feel that his class is an extension of his family.

We will be going into this in much greater detail in Chapters 2 and 5.

Maintaining a High-Quality Staff in the Face of Serious Obstacles in the Profession

It is axiomatic that teachers and administrators should be well trained in the field of early child development. In theory, this is so universally recognized that it should not be necessary to elaborate the point. Zero to Three puts particular emphasis on it, declaring, "The strongest indicators for long-term success . . . are related to the caregivers education and level of participation in ongoing training in the field of early child development and care. Staff competence is the most important contributing factor to a social environment that facilitates early learning. Caregivers should apply their knowledge of early childhood development and use curriculum and materials to plan appropriate activities and provide responsive caregiving."[45]

Nevertheless, despite its universal recognition as the core element in the success or failure of a child care center, professional development is one of the major problems in the profession. Training in a field such as this one must involve higher education, which is expensive and becoming even more so in recent years. Most college graduates these days leave academia with heavy student loans to repay. Few choose a profession with a salary level that hardly enables them to pay for rent, expenses, and a used car to get to and from work, let alone having to figure out how to pay back those loans.

Added to this is the fact that there are no uniform national standards for teachers of very young children. In addition to regular inspections by state authorities, Rosa Lee Young undergoes examination to gain accreditation from the National Association for the Education of Young Children, a nationwide professional organization. It is strictly a voluntary procedure on the part of the school and is obtained after observers from the NAEYC visit the school, observe the teachers, examine how the school is run, and approve the program. But professional requirements for staff vary from state to state and even within states. Many early child care centers require a two-year associate's degree, but there are some in which only a high school diploma is necessary to obtain a job.

In New York State, the minimum requirements for an early child care teacher is either an associate's degree in child development, recreation, or a related field with no additional experience or a high school diploma or its equivalent and two years of experience working with children under 13 years of age. It goes without saying that two years of working with 11- and 12-year-olds is hardly preparation for working with preschool age children. For a teacher's aide, New York State requires only a high school diploma or its equivalent and "substantial experience"

Bringing a Story to Life

The children in the prekindergarten class of Barbara Quinterno and Quinnale Drayton gathered around for circle time. Barbara sat on the floor with the children and gave a familiar signal for them to cross their legs. She had a book on the floor in front of her.

Barbara: Turn to your friend next to you. Shake his hand and say, "Hello. How are you?"

(After the children do this, she picks her arms up high over her head, gradually lowering them as her fingers flutter.)

Barbara: Let our fingers be leaves falling down. (The children imitated her.)

First child: I like pink.

Second child: I'm a little teapot.

(Barbara picks up a book about a scarecrow and talks to the children about scarecrows to introduce the book: what a scarecrow is, what it is used for, how it is made.)

Third child: (impatiently): Aren't you going to read the story?

Barbara (complying): It's time to listen. Now, I'm going to need your help. We're all going to be scarecrows and frighten away the birds so they don't eat the food the farmer is growing. Let's make scary faces to frighten away those birds.

(The children begin to make faces. Barbara then gives each child a number. As she reads the story, she signals them, using the children's assigned numbers, from time to time at an appropriate point in the story, to make scary faces to frighten the crows away. The children try to outdo each other in putting on scary faces, and the teacher joins them in the exercise as they practice being as silly as they can be.)

Barbara: Face Number 2 can even be meaner.

(Child Number 2 makes another scary face.)

Barbara: Oh, I think Face Number 3 didn't work. The birds are still there.

(Child Number 3 makes another face.)

(Barbara reads the point in the story where the birds are coming back to the field.)

Barbara: Let's also stamp our feet and make noise to scare the birds away.

(Children stamp feet and yell out as they make more scary faces.)

Barbara (after the story is finished): All right, the birds are gone. I don't see any. Let's put away our scary faces for a while. Shall we make our own scarecrows?

The children then followed up the story by making their own scarecrows with construction materials: paper, scissors, crayons, magic markers, and so on. They acted out the story, playing the roles of birds and scarecrows. Their art and construction work was then hung on the wall along with the highlights of the story itself so that, in effect, every child became a part of the story.

in working with children under 13. How substantial experience is interpreted apparently depends on the individual child care center. Some child care centers require college degrees and specific course training in early child care, but people willing to complete such requirements for a field with such small remuneration are hard to find. And even among those who enter the child care field, a large number leave it after only a few years seeking jobs in higher paying careers, leading to high staff turnovers. It is one of the more unfortunate aspects of the present administration of child care in this country. A study done a few years ago among 158 centers, for example, revealed that during the year 1997 alone, 27 percent of child care teachers and 39 percent of assistant teachers left their jobs, and 20 percent reported losing half or more of their teaching staff.[46]

Rosa Lee Young also has its problems in keeping staff salaries at a level commensurate with the education, training, and importance of the job. Although the school has made an effort to keep compensation at the highest level possible in the field, like nearly all other child care programs, it cannot escape the fact that it is run on a tight budget and that salaries are still admittedly very low when measured against other professions. "I would like to take care of our teachers better in terms of compensation," Director Rey lamented. She has discussed with the school's board of trustees the problem of attracting and keeping quality staff members. "The money hasn't kept up with the times in compensation and benefits," she admitted.

Nevertheless, in contrast to many child care center staffs, the Rosa Lee Young staff has, for the most part, been both educationally qualified and relatively stable. Several years ago, when I first began gathering material for this book, a survey of the staff revealed that five of the eight teachers had bachelor's degrees; three of them (including Pepper Robinson) had master's degrees in early childhood education. The other three had associate's degrees from community colleges. And rather than a high turnover, the teaching staff averaged nearly ten years at the school. One of them had taught there for twenty-three years, another for sixteen years. Three more had been teaching there for twelve, eleven, and ten years. Sadly, over the past couple of years, the rising cost of living and the inability of child care centers to keep up with the salary needs of its professional staffs have had their toll on Rosa Lee Young, as it has had on so many others. Several of its long-term staff members have left, usually for positions in public elementary schools. Pepper Robinson has received well-deserved recognition as an educator and now occupies the position of director at an early child care center in a town not far from Rockville Centre. So, even with a history of relative staff stability, the Rosa Lee Young program has also suffered from the problem that will remain chronic to the profession until it is accorded its proper place, with its proper remuneration, in our society.

How did the school manage to retain, at least by comparison with other early child care centers, a generally stable staff? When prekindergarten teacher Linda Schnitzer answered that question she could not contain her vibrancy.

"This is such a happy, encouraging, magical place," she declared. Seventeen years ago, she just happened to pass by the building and saw kids playing in the two outside play yards. "I didn't know this was a school," she recalled, because the sign outside was so small she missed it. A native of Rockville Centre with an associate's degree in early childhood education, she had lived elsewhere for a number of years but returned home when her father became ill. She was looking for a job in early childhood education, something "temporary until things got settled at home." She walked in, was interviewed by then-director Joan Sheppard, and was hired on the spot to fill the position of a teacher who was leaving because she would soon give birth. "In my mind I had no intention of staying," she recalled. So why did this temporary job turn into what has effectively become a lifetime occupation?

Linda had worked in a number of early child care centers for nine years before she came to Rosa Lee Young, but she "had never seen an early childhood program like this one. This was a place where children learn," she asserted, with a bursting exuberance. "This was a place where adults learn." It was at Rosa Lee Young, she said, where she learned how to teach.

On Linda's first day, Director Sheppard took her upstairs to her classroom where, after warming up to each other, the children wanted her to draw them a picture. As Linda began to draw the picture, Joan walked behind her and said softly, "Linda, why don't you ask Sally to show you how she would make it?"

"She was telling me that their philosophy was you don't draw pictures for children, you sit with them, and you encourage them to bring out their work," Linda said. That was different from where she had taught previously where "there were ditto sheets, there were teacher projects, every one the same," she went on. "When the children went home on Friday, it was important for the parents to see those ditto sheets with the alphabet and so forth. Every holiday was the same. On Halloween every child made a pumpkin. Even if a child didn't want to make a pumpkin, he made a pumpkin. If you told them to draw with the red pencil, they had to pick up the red pencil and draw in the red circle."

When she came to the school, Linda "was ignited. I said, 'Wow, this is teaching.' I saw such a difference in the way children played, and play in young children is very much a tool for learning."

The teachers at Rosa Lee Young create lesson plans, outlining the things that children are learning through specific play activities. If they make play dough, for example, they are learning science by observing the behavior of certain substances, they are learning math by measuring the ingredients, they are developing eye-hand coordination and muscles.

"Our parents know that with our philosophy, even though they may not see the ditto sheets, their children are learning in every area," Linda said.

Of course, as with good teaching on all levels, lesson plans provide a guide, but in practice the teacher is flexible enough to adapt a plan to specific needs and situations as they arise in a classroom. This is particularly true with young children who cannot follow a preset structure as easily as older children can and who are constantly learning through their own processes of experimentation and observation.

And the training at the school is ongoing. "It doesn't matter whether you have a master's degree or an associate's degree, you are continually training," Linda emphasized. "Staff meetings and team meetings discuss children and their specific needs so that the program is absolutely directed to the individual child."

Probably the biggest factor at Rosa Lee Young, Linda maintained, is the warm, supportive atmosphere among colleagues and administrators. If a child has a particular problem, whether it be "socializing, being able to problem solve, being able to retrieve words and recall situations, anything, you are encouraged to involve the administration so the child can receive appropriate help. If a teacher goes to the office, the social worker or director will always stop to talk to you, not just for children with special problems but any child or any situation that comes up in a classroom on a day-to-day basis and you need advice on how to handle the situation," Linda said.

This collegial atmosphere, this overall satisfaction with the work being done with children keeps qualified people at the center, even though they could probably earn much more elsewhere. For Linda Schnitzer, who saw children playing in the yard seventeen years ago as she was walking past the building, it has been what changed a stopgap job into a dedicated life career. And although she admitted, "The salary has been the hardest part of a job in this field," she said, "I absolutely would do it all over again." She sums up her years at Rosa Lee Young by stating simply, "I can't leave here. I just love it. It's a career that's definitely my spirit." Unfortunately, she finally did have to leave, forced out by health problems.

* * * * *

In this introductory chapter, we have outlined the general philosophy and qualities of what makes a good child care center and why this particular center seems to be working so well. We will be examining some other specific areas of a high-quality child care program in the chapters that follow.

We said at the outset that Rosa Lee Young inspired both hope and tragedy at the same time; hope because of the beauty of what good professional child care can do for the children of working parents, tragedy because there are not nearly enough Rosa Lee Youngs in America today. And as we observed the classes at the school, we could not help being consumed by the tragedy and the frustration over the current general state of early child care and what could be done with the proper resources. Frustration that in a nation whose leaders often proclaim that "children are our most precious resource," many people whose work is of dubious social value become wealthy, but teachers like Pepper Robinson are paid a pittance by comparison. Frustration and tragedy because what transpired in that toddler classroom was something like a work of great art. Though many would probably scoff at the idea, for me, seeing those teachers bringing out the best in those small children and giving them the foundation for a positive start in life was like watching great actors performing Shakespeare or listening to a Beethoven symphony. It was at once breathtaking and emotionally moving. It was great art because it was life; in its essence it showed what human beings were capable of doing when they had the training and the tools—and the heart and soul to do it.

What Are the Criteria That Make a Good Child Care Center?

1. Does the physical setup at the school conform to the basic standards of good practice for an early child care center as defined by national professional organizations like the National Association for the Education of Young Children or Zero to Three? Is the school fully accredited by the NAEYC?

2. Does each classroom have separate sections where children can go to play alone or in small groups, as well as a central space where the entire class can engage in activities together?

3. Does each class, from the toddler class to the prekindergarten and kindergarten classes, have materials that will engage children, encourage them to play, and stimulate their imaginations? These materials should include but not be limited to construction toys and puzzles, dolls and play furniture, painting supplies, playdough, water toys, housekeeping utensils, dress-up clothes, and musical instruments. Is there a playground with safe equipment for outdoor play?

4. Are toddlers and their parents welcomed at the school each morning in a way that makes daily separation much easier for the children? When they drop off their children, do parents get the chance to acknowledge the toddler's feelings of separation, remind them of where they will be during the day, and let them know when they will be back to pick them up?

5. Is the atmosphere of the child care center one that encourages an ongoing relationship of mutual trust among the children, their families, and the school? From the time the child starts the day, does the teacher establish an emotional connection with the child that leads to an atmosphere of trust and respect in the class?

6. When teachers read to children, do their voices and expressions reflect the tones and mood of the stories: animation, excitement, mirth, hushed tones, suspense, or whatever emotion the passage they are reading calls for? Are they really conveying the emotional content as well as the words to the children?

7. Are the means available for children to act out the stories they hear; for example, flannel boards, dress-up corners, puppets, dolls, toys, props? Are they encouraged to make up dances and body movements to the stories?

8. Is the teacher tuned in to the cues from the children that provide early signals as to how they feel about things such as the activity they're engaged in, their relationships with other children, when they are tired, or when they are overstimulated?

9. When working with toddlers, is the caregiver prepared for the reactions that come from the different emotional levels of the children? Does she allow for variations in personality when she plans her program? Does she anticipate that there will sometimes be inexplicable emotional outbursts from some of the children, and will she adjust her classroom routines to meet these needs?

10. When children express themselves, does the teacher ask questions that get them to think more deeply about what they have said?

11. When working with toddlers, does the teacher constantly interact and speak to them, using words to convey thoughts and emotions, even though she is aware that, unlike older children, the responses will not always be directly connected to the idea she expressed?

12. Are mealtimes at the school times for pleasant conversation around the table as the children eat?

13. Are activities planned and carried out in a manner that takes into account each child's unique personality and developmental level?

14. Is there more than the normal turnover in staff at the school?

A game at circle time.

The First Task
of Early Child Care

Building a Trusting Relationship
Between Caregiver, Child, and Family

When children are treated with respect, they conclude that they deserve respect and hence develop self-respect. When children are treated with acceptance, they develop self-acceptance; when they are cherished, they conclude that they deserve to be loved, and they develop self-esteem.

—Stephanie Martson

Children who are not spoken to by live and responsible adults will not learn to speak properly. Children who are not answered will stop asking questions. They will become incurious. And children who are not told stories and who are not read to will have few reasons for wanting to learn to read.

—Gail Haley

One of the first things very young children need is an attachment with a primary caregiver. The child's first primary caregiver is his mother, with whom he initially bonds. In an early child care program, the child's teacher becomes, in effect, the child's substitute parent for the day. In this chapter, using prekindergarten and kindergarten classes at Rosa Lee Young, we illustrate

- Why the teacher must successfully build this vital emotional attachment with the children in her care as the vital prerequisite to any kind of teaching that will take place
- How the teacher can create a developmentally appropriate environment, one that simultaneously fashions an atmosphere in the classroom that is both emotionally nurturing even as it stimulates learning
- How each child in a group situation can be made to feel unique
- Why flexibility is important in daily class routines
- The best way a teacher can deal with the problem of aggression in young children
- How the child care center can establish and maintain the link between school and home that is vital to the process of working successfully with children; how it can strengthen the important task of mutual respect and communication between parent, teacher, and administrators as partners in the healthful development of the children

The first time I saw Barry he was running around a classroom of 4-year-old preschoolers in a Manhattan child care center. It was obvious that he had a very hard time controlling himself. When he stopped running, he roamed around aimlessly, sometimes speaking to other children, at other times adopting an aggressive stance, fighting with them or kicking them. He paid little attention to the teacher, who was quite young and inexperienced herself and was generally overwhelmed by the number—she was in charge of twenty children. For most of the time, she was the only adult in the room, except for some even more inexperienced aides who alternately came in to help for a few minutes at a time throughout the day.

The program had been established with partial federal funding and was run by New York City. It was a poor setting for any child care program, particularly one in which a child like Barry was a part, because Barry came into that program with the label "at-risk child" practically stamped on his forehead. A highly active little boy with a round expressive face and large eyes that often reflected sadness and fear, he was born to a mother who had been on and off drugs for some time and who had never been able to establish with her child the loving attachment all infants and young children need. Although there were periods in which he seemed tranquil, he could not interact well with other children in the classroom and often was highly disruptive, even taking pleasure in hurting some of the other children.

My role as a child therapist was to visit the center twice a week, take out children who needed help, and meet with them in small groups in a smaller playroom setting. One of the groups consisted of Barry and two other children. In the small group, they would have the chance to initiate and play out their own symbolic themes. Through dramatic play and drawing pictures around themes—such as mommy, daddy, feeding children, going to the doctor, having little brothers and sisters, and even witnessing violence—they would be able to express much of the anxieties and problems they faced that they could not express in the regular classroom setting where the teacher was not able to give them the attention they needed. In the long run, it helped to make them feel better about themselves, relate to others, and be able to regulate themselves better in their classroom. Barry particularly liked to dance—as he moved to the music, some of his anxiety and aggression seemed to fade away for a few moments. In my work with them, I frequently became what the teacher could not be because of the size of the class and her lack of training: a substitute parent figure to whom they attached, enabling them to express their fears and their likes and dislikes in an atmosphere in which they felt accepted and safe. It was more difficult for Barry than for the other two in his group because Barry's problem was the lack of a secure attachment figure during the earliest years of his life. Although it was easier for the other two to form an attachment with me, it was much more difficult for Barry. Such an attachment is essential for a young child before anything else is possible.

Barry's problem is no longer an isolated one. Recent reports indicate that this problem is growing. A May 17, 2005, article in *The New York Times* reported on a study done by the Yale Child Study Center that showed a widespread number of expulsions of children from preschool programs. "No one wants to hear about 3- and 4-year-olds being expelled from preschool but it happens rather frequently," according to Walter S. Gilliam, the chief author of the study. Although the causes of the expulsions were not measured in the study, Gilliam said that they would have included a wide range of behaviors, such as aggression toward the teacher or other children or acts that might cause the teacher to worry about injury to the children and liability, like the child's running into the parking lot, according to *The Times* story. Some preschool directors maintained that they have seen a sharp rise since the 1970s in the number of children with behavioral problems. One director, an educational psychologist, noted, "In the past, in a school of 150 kids, you might have one or two kids with behavior problems, but now it may be up to 10 percent of the kids. In the past, many of these children weren't sent to school because their parents sensed they weren't ready." But now, there are so many more children who need child care, starting younger and staying longer hours.

The same *Times* story noted, "Expulsions were about twice as common in classrooms where the teachers had no access to a child psychologist or psychiatrist as in those where they did." In the cases of most of the children I worked with, their behavior problem decreased over the year in which I was able to become that attachment figure, filling in for just a couple of hours a week for a gaping void in their young lives. With Barry it didn't come until into the second year of our meetings. However, no follow-up study was done on these children and it is difficult to know how they fared later on.

"Schools are the place just beyond home where children wish to do well," observed Rebecca Shahmoon Shanok, director of the Institute for Infants, Children and Families in New York, "but too often feel bewildered, disoriented, overwhelmed, miserable, unpartnered, or completely alone, unable to traverse the gulf between home and school, unable to meet expectations. Yet, in school, supportive, individualized relationships can naturally be fostered with a young child, with teachers, and, very often, with parents as well. Building such developmentally attuned partnerships with parents and teachers enables them to do likewise with their children."[47]

ATTACHMENT, THE FIRST BASIC NEED OF ALL CHILDREN

Writing on this need of a child for attachment, renowned child psychiatrist Daniel J. Siegel and child development specialist Mary Hartzell observed in their book: "Babies are born into the world dependent upon their parents for their very survival. It is most often the mother, but can be another loving, sensitive caregiver, who initially provides food and comfort for the newborn and to whom the infant develops a primary attachment. . . . Attachment research points to the importance of the parent-child relationship in shaping children's interactions with other children, their sense of security about exploring the world, their resilience to stress, their ability to balance their emotions, their capacity to have a coherent story that makes sense of their lives, and their ability to create meaningful interpersonal relationships in the future. Attachment lays a foundation for how a child comes to approach the world, and a healthy attachment in the early years provides a secure base from which children can learn about themselves and others."[48]

All children need this attachment. For those entrusted with the care of young children, the lesson is obvious. Studies demonstrate, "A nurturing relationship with someone other than a parent in which the child feels understood and safe provides an important source of resilience, a seed in the child's mind that can be developed later on as the child grows. Relationships with relatives, teachers, childcare providers, and counselors can provide an important source of connection for the growing child. These relationships don't replace a secure attachment with a primary caregiver, but they are a source of strength for the child's developing mind."[49]

Or, as the noted author and scholar on child development Alice Honig observed, "Building a secure attachment is a prime goal in early child care and education; it is in fact the keystone for ensuring children's sound mental health. . . . A secure attachment in the child care setting can be a lifesaver for an abused or neglected infant, and it is a plus for all children."[50] Before any progress can be made with a child, before that child can learn how to play and share with other children, before she can express herself meaningfully or recognize pictures and letters and words, the child must form a strong attachment with an adult human being who will make her feel safe and secure. If she already has one at home, then the child care provider in whose charge she is for a good portion of the day becomes her attachment figure for that time she spends in school, substituting for her mother during those hours. A child can be attached to more than one adult caregiver, and a good previous attachment with her mother and her memories of that close personal relationship can provide the basis for a good additional attachment in a child care situation.

This is especially true when working with children who have not had the nurturing of loving parents before they come into child care and who subsequently exhibit special problems in behavior and adjustment. It is often forgotten that every young child has already developed a personality based upon his previous three or four or five years of experience. A child care center has to be aware of this fact when confronting a child whose behavior is more difficult than that of other children and that this problem has root causes that have to be understood if the child is to be worked with successfully.

As much as it is true for children who have missed that attachment and therefore pose a problem, *it's true for all children, including the ones from the most secure homes and the most loving, caring parents.* This is because although the child's relationship with the parent should always be her most important one, her attachment with other adults "can strengthen the parent-child bond as well as offer more opportunities for children to experience supportive, nurturing relationships." Thus summarized Rebecca Parlakian in her work on how to best prepare children for learning from their earliest years. She wrote:

> Such relationships with parents and others have been associated with greater self-confidence and self-motivated learning during the toddler years. As in parental relationships, when these interactions are supportive, responsive, and nurturing, children begin to develop trust, empathy, compassion, generosity, and a conscience. Research shows that healthy adult-child relationships provide a context for supporting children's growing sense of self-direction, curiosity, persistence, cooperation, caring, and conflict-resolution. These social-emotional skills help children first to approach school with confidence and optimism, then to successfully adjust to the academic environment.

Citing the conclusion of a recent study that the single most critical component to quality child care rests in the relationship between the child and the teacher/caregiver, and in the ability of the adult to be responsive to the child, Parlakian stressed that parents and child care professionals make important contributions to children's school readiness. For infants and toddlers, care and education are not separate activities. They occur together, one leading to the other, one supporting the other.[51]

An interesting follow-up to the *New York Times* article appeared in the same paper a few days later. It quoted some child development professionals as laying major cause for the difficult behavior in many preschool children to the recent emphasis on academic-centered preschooling, that is, getting kids to learn to sit and write and count at the age of 3 rather than performing what should be the principal task of preschool: creating confidence and security in the child and attachment to his caregivers and building the child's social skills in order to prepare him to learn. The recent stress on academics, on pushing alphabet drills and number drills on children before they are ready for it, comes in the wake of the passage of federal legislation that pressures states and local school systems to meet tough new academic standards enforced by testing from the earliest grades. This has put pressure on preschools to push academics at the expense of child development, often with nervous parents demanding that early child care teach academics so their child is not left behind.[52]

"An enormous amount of energy has been invested recently in assessing the academic status of children in the early grades," noted Lesley Koplow. "Determining young children's reading ability has been a special focus of this attention: Many programs have been put in place to pinpoint a child's reading level immediately on entering school so that he or she can be stimulated accordingly." But this, she warns, may be misplaced. "We are attempting to assess academic capacity in 4- to 7-year-olds instead of assessing the social and emotional underpinnings of that capacity. Along the road to personhood, many children face enormous challenges that they cannot overcome alone. . . . Sometimes we know nothing about the challenges that a child has faced before coming to school, but we are soon living with the results of those challenges, which create havoc or paralysis in the classroom."[53]

We will be examining this phenomenon in greater detail, including the best way of preparing children to learn in school, in Chapter 6.

The point that has been repeatedly stressed by the most knowledgeable people in the field of early child care is thus a very clear one. *It is that no child can learn anything, not cognitively, not emotionally, not socially, unless she has a loving, trusting relationship with an adult caregiver. Before she can learn how to share things with others or to take turns at an activity or to share joyful or sad experiences with others or to read or to add or subtract, she must know that the person who is teaching her these things is someone upon whom she can rely, who will be a solid rock in her young life.*

No young child can learn without this firm foundation of love and caring. If the early childhood teacher, who sees the child for the better part of most days, carries forward the work of the parent and provides this solid foundation, the child will go on and learn for the rest of his life. If instead, she tries to function as a "dispenser of knowledge" to the young child, all the reading and math drills and all the discipline measures she gives to the child on his social and emotional behavior will amount to very little.

The primary task facing an early child care program in its work with toddlers and preschoolers seems self-evident. It is to create a *developmentally appropriate environment* for them during the time they are at the center. What exactly do we mean by *developmentally appropriate* environment and practices for this age group? It means, according to one prominent scholar and practitioner in the field, "creating a caring community of learners, one that is inclusive, safe, and orderly and emphasizes social relationships. It means teaching to enhance development and learning by respecting children's individual differences, fostering collaboration among peers, facilitating development of self-regulation, and structuring an intellectually engaging and varied environment." It also means, she adds, "establishing reciprocal, supportive relationships with

Mr. Snowman.

families, including sharing information, supporting families in times of stress, linking them with support services, and recognizing the complexity and importance of the shared responsibility in child-rearing."[54] In short, the early child care center's first job is to provide a loving and meaningful setting and attachment for the child that allows him to grow and develop.

CREATING A STIMULATING AND NURTURING ATMOSPHERE IN THE CLASSROOM

Keeping this squarely in mind, let's turn to Rosa Lee Young. Barbara Quinterno, a teacher in one of the two prekindergarten classes, has been at Rosa Lee Young for several years. A generally reserved woman, her face lights up and her personality bursts forth when she is in class with her children. Suddenly she is an animated teacher reading a story about trees that move in the wind, or show-ing the children how to make designs on paper by blowing paint with their breaths through a straw, or listening sympathetically to a child who didn't want to take her afternoon nap. If you want an illustration of how an early childhood educator builds secure relationships with children, Barbara's class is a good place to begin.

Teachers at Rosa Lee Young use many different approaches, but the object is the same. The classes are well organized and structured, but loose enough to allow children a great deal of flexibility for their individual needs and desires. There is a beginning, the greeting to each child in the morning as he arrives; a middle, the varied activities during the day; and an end, at circle time in the afternoon. I observed Barbara Quinterno's class on a Monday morning as some of the children were still not readjusted after the weekend to another week of early rising.

The school opens its doors at 7:30 a.m. to accommodate working parents who have to drop their children off early. Tjuana Evans, who is actually in charge of food service and has been a familiar and loved figure at the school for about a dozen years, greets the small number of early arrivals as they come in one by one, singing with them, giving some of them breakfast if they want it, engaging in circle games and conversation until the regular teachers arrive at 8:30. When Barbara came in, there were five children from her class of fifteen already there. Barbara's associate teacher, Phoebe Pantaleon, arrives later and stays later in the afternoon to accommodate parents who work later hours.

Barbara greeted each child. Some of them were still yawning. Barbara rec-ognized this with animated expressions of sympathy: "Oh, I know how you feel. It's Monday morning and you're still tired. Let's just relax for a while." She sat down on the floor, joining the children in a group. "Criss-cross, applesauce," she said, and the children knew the signal to cross their legs on the floor. "What did you do this weekend?" One child began talking about his weekend experi-ences. As the class filled up between 8:30 and 9:00, each new child joined the group, and each, in turn, chimed in about his own doings since Friday. As they spoke, they eased into the friendly atmosphere of the class and the routine with which they were familiar. When some of them became restless, Barbara was alert to it and easily went into a movement mode, saying, "Let's shake our sil-lies out. Julia would you like to lead the class?" Julia, who loves to move about in rhythmic patterns, then led the children as they moved around the area shak-ing their bodies.

Then came sharing time. Each child was encouraged to bring something to share with the class and the teacher. Tyler brought a small ball. "Is the ball big or little?" asked Barbara, and the children answered. Barbara then compared it with the larger ball she had on the shelf and talked about how soft and squeezy and what pretty colors Tyler's ball was. Paul shared a story. "I'm going to Florida to Mickey Mouse castle," he said. Julia brought in two pictures, one when she was a baby and one when she was a year old. She then talked about how she had her hair braided over the weekend. Other children also shared objects or experiences. When a child didn't have any particular thing to show or say, Barbara would say, "You'll tell us about it later." When a child began talking while another child was doing the sharing, the teacher said gently, "You have to be quiet so your ears can hear what she's saying." At one point a child put his leg across another child as they sat on the floor and the second child didn't like it. "Just tell him don't put your leg across my body," she counseled. All of it was done to create a sense of dignity and worth of each child, important textbook principles of early childhood education carried out in simple daily routines in a classroom.

HOW CAN A TEACHER HANDLE AGGRESSION IN CHILDREN?

We began this chapter with a story about Barry, a child who often acted aggressively toward other children because of his own troubled background. We are often disturbed when children are aggressive. In a classroom situation or in play with other children, a child's aggressiveness usually raises concern because it can cause friction with other children, disruption in the smooth operation of the class, and a reversal of the positive peer relationships the teacher is trying to build. There are children like Barry whose troubled background can lead to serious problems for himself and others, both in and out of the classroom. But not all aggressive behavior comes from troubled children. Those who work with children must take into consideration whether the aggression is one in which a child occasionally is reacting spontaneously to a particular situation or part of a pattern.

Stanley I. Greenspan, a leading authority on young children, tells us that aggression in children is perfectly normal sometimes and that the problem is often not the aggression, but the way adults are trained to handle it.

> Oddly enough, the appearance of aggressive themes in your child's pretend play and conversation (at about three to four years of age) can be another sign of developmental progress. As parents we want to foster feelings that fuel assertiveness and a healthy interest in power, yet control the acting out of aggression in which a child might hit, hurt, or break things. You'll see constructive uses of aggressiveness during your child's pretend play, when she takes on the role of the biggest and most powerful superhero who cuts the bad guys down to size, or becomes the most beautiful and talented ballerina in the company. You'll also notice when aggressiveness enters into her conversations with you, as she forcefully states her own point of view. Most parents try to promote this quality in their children; they don't want them to be timid or passive. They want their children to feel comfortable raising their hands in school, volunteering, participating in discussions, and holding their own during a debate.
>
> All children need opportunities for assertiveness, and rely on you to set behavioral limits that will keep their impulsive acting out in check. . . . It's important to recognize that you must offer your child

some avenues of assertiveness. You want to help her use her words to elaborate *all* the themes of life, from power and assertiveness to sweetness and loving-kindness. If you cut out all areas of assertiveness from her experience, you'll be undermining a very important part of her emotional life. . . . There are many ways within a variety of cultural and religious traditions to express assertiveness and to experiment with power using words and imaginative play. . . . Try not to overreact when your four-year-old becomes temporarily preoccupied with these aggressive themes. Each time she imagines herself to be bigger, stronger, and faster than the scariest creature that haunts her, she regains a sense of control over her life.[55]

Take for example, an episode I witnessed in one class. During the free activity time, Sarah and Michelle were playing separately in the family corner. Michelle was holding a doll as her baby and rocking her to sleep in her arms when Sarah picked up another doll and then took a plastic toy knife and began trying to cut the doll up. The teacher saw the action and spoke to the girl gently. The following brief dialogue ensued between them:

Teacher: Are you a good mommy or a bad mommy? Are you being kind to that baby? You have to be gentle with her. What are you doing with the knife?

(Child hesitates, slowing down her cutting motion)

Teacher: You're hurting her. Hug her. Be nice to her.

(Child hugs the doll).

Teacher: Doesn't it feel nice? (Sarah nods and walks away still holding the doll).

The teacher in this case did not become disturbed or get angry at the child's behavior. Her voice was soft when she told the child to hug the doll instead of cut it. Her treatment of Sarah was loving, caring, and accepting even as she was directing the girl into more acceptable behavior. In Sarah's case it could have been simply an isolated incident caused by some temporary frustration, or it could have been a sign of a more serious behavioral problem, but either way the teacher must resist her natural impulse to react with shock or horror, or take punitive measures. If the child had more serious problems, these were more than likely caused by negative experiences with aggressive, punitive adults and with failure to receive nurturing and love in the earlier years. An overreaction by an adult would only reinforce that image in the child's mind and compound the problem, leading to more aggressive behavior as a means of self-protection.

In this case the teacher could have even gone further. She could have asked, "Why are you cutting that baby with the knife?" a question that might elicit from the child reasons for her behavior. How, why, and when questions are often very useful in getting the child to organize her thoughts more clearly about her action. The teacher could have entered into the child's play situation by asking who the doll is, what happened to make Sarah so angry at the doll, could the doll become her friend, and so on. As one prominent child psychologist pointed out, when the adult enters into the play situation with the child, he helps the child "develop the tools to make sense of things, to link experiences together, and to unravel the tangle of feelings and impulses. . . . And by playing with the child, we become part of the child's discovery of what he or she means to say and means to feel."[56]

Carrying the play still further, the teacher might have asked Sarah, "How does it feel when you cut the baby with a knife? The baby loves you and wants you to hug her, not hurt her. How does it feel when you hug the baby?"

Of course, with a class of other children needing attention, it is not always possible to deal with one child in this way, which is why a favorable teacher-pupil ratio is so necessary, particularly among very young children. And children like Barry, who are abnormally aggressive and manifest major behavior problems, usually need special help beyond what the classroom teacher is equipped to give. But people who work with children in these situations must be able to handle them in a professional manner, which often means that they suppress their natural desire to meet aggressive behavior with shock and aggression of their own. They must keep in mind that their mission is to build a trusting relationship with the child, helping him to overcome his difficulties to the greatest extent they are able.

FLEXIBILITY AND THE ADULT-CHILD RELATIONSHIP: WHY RULES AND SCHEDULES NEED TO BE ADAPTED

As with the work of most dedicated teachers, Barbara Quinterno's work with children doesn't end when she leaves the class—her concern carries over into professional meetings and planning and often in thinking and worrying about some of her children.

She expressed her concern about one of them, a 4-year-old named Susan, in a discussion at a staff meeting one day. I had been invited by the director, Jeannine Rey, to participate in the meeting's main discussion topic, what constitutes a quality early childhood center. After a discussion of some basic principles, the teachers talked about how these principles could be implemented in their classrooms and then about the best ways to work with some of the children in their classes with special problems.

Tuning in to Susan

Susan is often on Barbara's mind. She has a great deal of difficulty interacting with the other children, frequently yelling and having tantrums in class. She often shows little interest in what is going on in the class. Her behavior can have an effect on the other young children in a social situation like a classroom, where some have at times also tended to emulate Susan. A child like Susan needs a great deal of one-on-one attention, Barbara noted, and you have to have a great deal of flexibility in dealing with her.

Take the regular afternoon nap time, for example. In other child care centers I have seen, this time is an absolutely rigid hour or two during which the children lie on their cots or floor mats and nap. If they don't want to sleep, they still must stay on their cots and play by themselves—but they can't get off until nap time is over.

But what if there is a child with a real problem, a child who needs personal attention more than the rest do? All children need a rest period in the afternoon, but what if a child needs some one-on-one with an adult on a particular afternoon more than that nap? Flexibility is one of the key elements in working with a child like Susan, and Barbara Quinterno obviously knows it.

On one particular afternoon, she told the meeting, Susan refused to lie down on her mat. Barbara decided to take her over to a chair and speak with her. The little girl is Hispanic and doesn't know much English, but suddenly expressed the desire, by pointing to objects, to learn more English. So the two of them played a game during nap time. As the girl pointed to the objects and said their names in Spanish, Barbara named them in English, and the girl repeated their names in both languages. Now, in doing this, Barbara was violating the principle of the block of nap time that is a solid rock in most early child care programs. But in this case, she was engaged in a far more important principle—and it was more than just teaching a little girl some English. The child was yearning for one-on-one contact with an adult that she loved and trusted. She wanted to talk and confide in someone and be held and comforted. And Barbara, as a teacher who was tuned in to her children, knew it and adapted the usual procedure for a day.

That is also one of the cardinal indications of a good childhood center. Expressed very simply, does the child come first or the organizational schedule? That's the impression that hit me the most as I watched each class in action at Rosa Lee Young. It was the many ways in which the teacher sought to build up a feeling that this class was a place where the children found warmth and support. One important way this was done was to get the children to understand that they could express their emotions freely, verbally or through art or symbolic play. If a child was sad or angry, he was encouraged to say so and to say why. Or if he could not express himself verbally, he could play it out or draw it. Whatever his emotion at a particular time, whether happiness or sadness or anger at another child or anything else, he was treated with respect and attention. He knew that he could always trust the teacher, his shelter and his strength, for the time he was there. There is a simple theoretical principle behind this practice. The more a child (or even an adult for that matter) is capable of expressing his emotions, particularly anger or frustration verbally or symbolically, the more a child can talk about what's bothering him, or play it out with a doll or a puppet or a picture or any other symbolic object, the less likely he is to act out violently or engage in destructive acts. This is the first step toward the socialization process in young children, an important step in preparing them for school. This is what people knowledgeable in the field of early child development look for when they observe preschool classes in action. And it's something that hits you directly when you visit a class at Rosa Lee Young.

BUILDING HUMAN RELATIONSHIPS IN EVERY CLASSROOM

Lisa Streb and Sally Ann Braman taught a prekindergarten and kindergarten class at the school. (Lisa has since left the school.) So many things were always going on in their class that it was often difficult to know just where to begin. But let's start with the simple rule to which this chapter is devoted—that the first job of preschool is to establish warm, nurturing relationships with young children and to make them feel good about themselves. In doing so the school is building up two vital strengths for a child's future, a belief in herself and her abilities and a spirit of cooperation and sharing with others that is necessary for success in school and in life. A visit to Lisa and Sally's class provided a host of examples of this.

On the day I came into the class, one of the children—a little boy named Richard, who normally was quite lively and alert—appeared extremely listless. He didn't play or move about with the other children as he usually did but instead sat still or stretched out on the floor. The child was not physically ill, but just needed some extra emotional support at that point.

Another child, a girl named Debra, was tall and physically mature for her tender age of 4, but immature in other ways. Because of her physical stature, she could exercise a degree of dominance over other children, but she needed

Learning to read with a hug.

Positive Touch: Something All Children Need

Beginning in the mid-1980s and continuing into the next decade, newspapers were full of stories of sexual abuse allegedly perpetrated by some child caregivers against children in their care. In New Jersey some were convicted and received prison sentences. Some of those convictions were later overturned and the defendants freed after serving prison time when it was determined that the evidence was highly dubious, at best, and that the children, in many cases, had been coached in their responses. Nevertheless, the big scare that ensued had child care teachers and administrators very nervous about the practice of touching or hugging children. Their fear that such "hugs, cuddles, and pats on the back in early child care settings . . . may be misconstrued or misinterpreted" led to a marked decline in the use of loving touch as a means of establishing a warm relationship between the caregiver and the children.

Child abuse is a very serious matter and vigilance must be maintained by child care institutions so that individuals who engage in such practices are not allowed to work with children. But there is obviously a big difference between proper and improper touching of children. "When teachers understand what touches children generally find comfortable and inoffensive and understand that programs can help protect children from abuse, they can adjust their behavior so that touching children in early childhood settings maintains its appropriateness and effectiveness." When early childhood educators over the past couple of decades were told by their schools not to touch the children, the school was denying the children what is really an essential part of their development.

All infants and young children need to be touched in a positive and loving way. This fact has been documented in countless studies by pediatric psychologists and psychiatrists. It is the most basic of all their senses. For example, child psychotherapist Lesley Koplow, who directs the Center for Emotionally Responsive Practice at Bank Street College of Education in New York, wrote, "Children who have not had opportunities to attach to a consistent, nurturing adult cannot develop well and are often difficult, inattentive, and disruptive in the classroom" and "for early-grade children, the most positive communicator of warmth and caring is touch." She cites one study of an elementary school program that instituted a "positive touch" policy in which the principal received children in the morning as they entered the building and hugged those who looked upset. The study reported that "incidents of child-to-child aggression in the building decreased by 46 percent and that test scores increased dramatically."

Of course, teachers must take into account "the child's culture, past experience with touching, and individual comfort level with touching" as well as the child's "level of attachment and sensory functioning." But positive touch, which includes hugs and other expressions of love, is an essential part of the emotional connection between the young child and his teacher in an early child care setting.

See Carlson, F. M. (2005, July). Significance of touch in young children's lives. *Young Children: Journal of the National Association for the Education of Young Children*, (pp. 79–85), and Koplow, L. (2002). *Creating schools that heal: Real life solutions*, (pp. 132, 133). New York: Teachers College Press.

help emotionally. She found it difficult to sit or engage in one activity for any length of time and often went to the teachers for calming. But Debra had a particular strength. She had begun to read, more than the other children read. She could read some of the books the teachers read to the class. So Sally solved two problems at once on this particular day. She knew that Debra, like most children, loved to exhibit her strength and be complimented for it. Sally had given her a book to take home to practice so she could read it aloud to the class. Now, Sally found the perfect time for it. As the class gathered for story time, she asked Debra if she would like to read the story to the class. What a sense of pride and accomplishment in this little girl as she showed her ability to read the story! And while she read the story, Sally sat on the floor and soothed Richard, holding him around, for a time gently scratching his back and making him feel that someone cared for him. The example set by the teacher was picked up by the other children. Children learn by examples, good and bad. One of the other boys, Gilbert, came over and put his arm around Richard. Others expressed their concern.

Another girl, Isabelle, also tall and mature for her age, had problems relating to the other children, often losing control of herself in the classroom, running around and disrupting the activities of the other children. Sally related that when this happened, they try to deal with it without admonition or blame, often just advising the child to take deep breaths or go to the bathroom sink and splash water on her face to calm herself down. The teachers and the social worker had recommended that the child be referred for some social services provided by the county, but her parents resisted.

Respect for the children is also always shown in simple language from the teacher, with soft, gentle commands and requests that guide the children, never forgetting the "please" and the "thank you." It is shown in the way the teacher gets children to slow down for periods of calm or rest—instead of telling them or commanding them, she simply dims the classroom lights a bit. The children have been taught to recognize the signal and react better than they would to a voice command. It is shown in the ways the teachers enlist the help of the children in the tasks of the classroom, making it a sense of sharing and responsibility of all. Listed on the wall are the jobs that each child takes care of for the week, his role in helping the class to run. The jobs change each week. And always, it is expressed as, "Roger, can you help put away the toys?" or, "Christina, can you help put the breakfast on the table?" When helping with the simple classroom chores, which are rotated each week, the children are assigned a title:

- Pet feeder: feeds pets, hamsters, and goldfish
- Table washer: washes tables after meals and snacks
- Calendar helper: tells class each day what day and month it is, what the weather is like, and other facts
- Line leader: the person who leads the line when the class goes out to the playground or to the library or whenever they leave the classroom

- Garbage helpers: several children who help to clean up breakfast, lunch, and snacks
- Flag holder: the child who gets to hold the flag while the children pledge allegiance
- Milk helpers: several children who help to distribute milk to the children
- Plant waterer: the child responsible for watering the plants in the classroom each day
- Librarian: the child in charge of collecting the books and making sure they are put away in an orderly manner
- Errand helper: the child who takes a note to another teacher or to the office when staff members have to communicate with each other during the day

These tasks go a long way toward creating a wholesome atmosphere in the classroom. They give the children the sense that their class, their teacher, and their classmates are a shared responsibility. They give the children simple jobs they can accomplish and a feeling that they can be successful and gain approval at accomplishing them. They also allow the teacher to make allowances for the different needs of individual children in assignment of the tasks at hand. It is all part of building a relationship with each child that is the first building block toward further growth and development.

The building of human relationships in the interactions between children and adults seems to be omnipresent in every classroom, even as they are engaged in activity that prepares them for school later on. In Lisa and Sally's class, for example, as all this is transpiring, the children are given a project for the week each Friday, to be brought in on Monday. This project assignment is given to the parents when they pick up the children on Friday afternoon, and the parents are encouraged to help the children in their assignment. On the week I was there, they were engaged in a scientific experiment. They had to cut and paste or draw things that were *cold*. Assisted by their parents, they drew, cut or pasted ice cubes, bottles of milk, soda, water from a tap, and a bunch of other things. They also had three other suggested activities they could do at home that called upon them to observe and talk about their experiences.

- Put an ice cube in a cup and leave it on a table overnight. What happened?
- Look outside for things that are blue. How many things do you see? What are they?
- Read a book with an adult. Talk to the class about your favorite part of the book.

These are simple things that get a child to observe and express himself but so important in preparing him for reading and learning that will take place for the rest of his life. In some early child care centers, the pressure for learning is so great that teachers prepare homework assignments based on ditto sheets to teach letters, numbers, and so forth. That type of formal lesson is shunned at

Rosa Lee Young and with good reason—the children are simply too young for it. But learning and academic preparation for school is an integral part of the program, even as the teachers accomplish the most important task of building self-confidence in the individual child, human warmth and trust between the child and his adult mentors, and cooperation and friendship among the children.

Hugging a Child Expresses What Words Often Cannot

Take the prekindergarten class several years ago of Linda Schnitzer and Vanessa Weiss-Barkofsky. Linda had been out for three weeks with a health-related problem. I visited the class on the first day of her return.

The children could not hide their glee at seeing her. It was obvious that the 3- and 4-year-olds had formed an attachment to her that was not broken by her absence. A big reason for this was that she called the school each day she was out and left messages for the children. Vanessa, her coteacher, in turn asked the children for messages to give to Linda, and these were related to her when she called. Thus she kept contact with the class for the entire time she was out. When she returned, she greeted each child and each one welcomed her with broad smiles. "Hello, Billy. Good morning, Philip. Hi, Samir." Each child got a personal greeting. Samir, a child of Indian parentage, went over to her and gave her a big hug. Linda responded with big hugs for Samir and the other children.

In fact, one thing that stood out about the class was the extent to which the teachers used the warmth of touch and hugs to convey the sense of love and attachment to the children. In recent years, this has been a problem in some places. I remember that at one child care center at which I worked back in the late eighties and nineties we were told, "Don't touch the children." This came out after a rash of cases hit the headlines back then over alleged sexual abuse of the children by child caregivers. (See box on page 43.)

But it was not a problem in this class. Hugs and expressions of love and warmth prevailed throughout the day. When addressing the children, the teachers conveyed respect for each child. That respect was reflected toward the teacher and toward other students. It was done in simple ways like using the words "sorry" and "thank you" as well as in more complicated situations in which children had disagreements. When one child reported, "Carson spit on me," Linda let Carson know that this was not right, but she did it in a soft way, teaching him to control his emotions but not admonishing him in such a way that the child lost his sense of security in the class. "You must be very angry," she said softly, "but we don't spit on our friends. We understand that, don't we?" The child seemed to understand and accept it.

In another incident two children were at play when one of them, a boy named Robert, got carried away and raised his voice suddenly to a decibel that was uncomfortable in the confines of the classroom. Loud yelling has a disconcerting effect upon young children and often tends to disrupt the normal calm of a classroom. Vanessa became upset and raised her voice too, telling the child sharply, "Lower your voice." As soon as she did this, she realized that it was not the best way of handling the situation. She took the child around, kissed him, and calmed him down. By performing this simple act, she was telling him, in effect, that yes, we're all human and we sometimes raise our voices, but the important thing is we love you and we think you're great.

When a child left one activity for another very quickly and Linda didn't want him to jump around too much, she didn't order him back. Instead, she went to his original spot and asked in a slightly surprised manner, "Did you change your mind?" and demonstrated some of the toys there to stimulate his interest. After considering, he came back and rejoined the group at the original activity. When a dispute developed between two children the emphasis of the teacher was not on blame or guilt, but encouraging them to negotiate their difference. "What can you do?" "Is there a better way to solve this problem?"

Whenever Vanessa went to another group of children, she greeted each child individually, asking, "What did you do this weekend?" or commenting on how nice a child looked, or how good he was at the task he was doing. In each group, she sat on the floor playing with them for a while. In one group she spotted a child bothering another child, a potential for a dispute, and simply said to the first child, "Do you need a hug?" The child came to her and was hugged as Vanessa said, "Of course you do."

THE UNDERLYING CLASS THEME:
WE ARE ALL PEOPLE AND I AM SOMEBODY

At one point in the class, as the children were absorbed in their activity groups, Linda and Vanessa sat together on the floor of the classroom talking about the class activities for the upcoming period. Two special activities revolved around the books *Caps for Sale* and *Bread, Bread, Bread*. The *Caps for Sale* story described all sorts of caps and hats, and the children followed up the story by making and wearing hats, from witches hats to spring bonnets and everything in between. After reading the story about bread, they made bread from different countries around the world. On St. Patrick's Day, they mixed the ingredients for Irish soda bread, which they then took to the kitchen and watched as the bread was placed in the oven and again as it was taken out, a finished product. On other days they did the same with Jewish challah bread, English muffins, Italian and French bread, and others. In addition to *Bread, Bread, Bread*, they read *Bread Comes to Life* and talked about the breads, the countries they came from, and the people and cultures who produce them.

The atmosphere they strive for in this class as well as the others is that their classroom is a family atmosphere, an extension of the child's own family. In addition to displaying the work of the children in the class, the bulletin boards are filled with pictures of the families of the children. When one child cried a bit for "her mommy," the teacher took her over to the board to show her the familiar face of her mommy and said to her soothingly, "Mommy's in the dentist's office" (her mother was a dental technician). "She dropped you off this morning and will pick you up later today." The children, from the earliest days at Rosa Lee Young, are encouraged to develop an identity, to see themselves as their own persons. From the folders belonging to each of them with their names attractively lettered on each, to their own cubbies in which they store the projects they're working on, to the coat hooks all bearing their names, everything at the school gives each child the message, "I am somebody."

MAKING PARENTS WELCOME: AN ESSENTIAL COMPONENT OF THE RELATIONSHIP BETWEEN CAREGIVER AND CHILD

As we have previously written, the establishment of a trusting relationship between the parent and the child care program is essential to the establishment of a trusting relationship between the professional caregiver and the child. One of the guiding principles of Rosa Lee Young is to do everything it can to make parents feel as much at home as the children themselves do.

Establishing the Parent-School Link Right From the Beginning

Before a child comes into the program, when the parent is simply considering sending her to Rosa Lee Young, the parent is invited to tour the building, observe the classrooms, and watch the children in action during the normal course of a school day. It isn't just a superficial look-see. "We give them an experience," said Jeannine Rey, "and from that they see things, they make comments, they ask questions, and we engage in a discussion of the program." When parents decide to enroll their children in the center, they sit down with Barbara Andrzejewski, the school social worker, for a two-hour intake interview. It covers a whole range of subjects—not just the usual administrative ones like policies and procedures, tuition, the holidays on which the school is closed, what a parent should do when a child is sick, who can pick the child up when the parent can't, and so forth. More important, Barbara goes through a child's history with the parent. She gets to know about the child's development, and asks family questions. Who lives in the household? Are there pets? Has the child ever experienced the death of anyone—a person or a pet? How does the parent handle discipline? She also goes into the family's preferences about food; for example, if they observe dietary laws because of religion or if they have any other restrictions. This is particularly important in a school like Rosa Lee Young, which strives to maintain a group of children from diverse racial, class, and religious backgrounds, as we describe in detail in Chapter 5.

"We had a family once, very health conscious, who didn't want their child to eat anything that came out of cans," recalled Jeannine. " It's sometimes difficult for our small kitchen, but we try." The school makes sure that a weekly menu is published ahead of time and sent home to the parents so they can see what the children are eating for their breakfasts, lunches, and snacks. If parents

An Important Family Event

Ongoing communication between the child care center and families can often be on top-
ics that range from the extraordinary to the mundane, and sometimes it's difficult to distinguish the difference. Consider the following:

The older sister of a toddler at Rosa Lee Young had her first Holy Communion over
the weekend. Early Monday morning the school's director greeted the toddler and his
father as the child was being dropped off at school. The following exchange ensued:

Director: You had an exciting event at your house over the weekend.

Dad (with pride): Yeah, a pee-pee in the toilet.

don't want a certain food for their child, they can bring in another one to substitute for it when they drop the child off in the morning.

Beyond this, the school takes active efforts to facilitate regular communication, beginning with the child's first day at the school. Teachers and staff recognize that separation anxiety is one of the major problems facing young children
in child care, and they deal with it directly. When the child is first admitted,
there is a long transitional period of adjustment. On the first day the child is in
class, the parent stays there for the entire day. The teacher uses the parent's
presence to talk with the parent and often the school's director and other professional staff members do the same. This does more than just exchange information. The child sees the parent, the teacher, and the staff members in friendly
conversation, and it enhances his confidence in the school. If necessary, this full
day with the parent is repeated until it is judged that the parent can leave the
child for a half day. Gradually the parent's time in the child's class is dimin-
ished until it is felt that the child is comfortable enough to be able to participate
in this friendly environment on his own. During this transition time, the parent
gets to see how the school operates, is encouraged to ask questions, and is made
to feel that she and her child belong.

Constant Communication Between Parent and School

The staff at Rosa Lee Young has developed a number of other techniques to
keep the lines of communication with parents open, although with so many of
their parents holding down full-time jobs, it is not always easy to find the time.
Nevertheless, this communication is essential to any successful child care program. To make the parents feel that they are welcome at the school cannot be
overstated. "I knew everybody by their first names. You always felt as if you
were leaving your children with a friend, a good friend, a competent friend,"
reported Ann Chin, a junior high school teacher whose two sons attended Rosa

Lee Young more than twenty years earlier. "There was never any hostility—ever. The director, the teacher, and I spoke all the time. We would chat about this and that, and, of course, about my child who was attending the school at the time. There was a newsletter published by the teacher, and if necessary, she would speak to me personally about one of my sons. You knew that the door was always open to you and you were at home in this building."

Each morning when the children are dropped off and in the late afternoons when they are picked up, the school staff makes it a point of talking for a minute or two with the parent, asking how everything is, telling the parent of some accomplishment the child had done recently, exchanging notes and tidbits. "We don't want them to just drop their children off at the door and leave," Jeannine said. "We want them to come in, come talk, come tell us about anything that's relevant to the child that happened since yesterday." The staff carries that policy through "with informal conversations with the parent whenever they can, and with parent-teacher conferences." If necessary, or if there is a more serious problem, there is a follow-up conference with the school social worker. In addition, teachers have a notebook near the teacher's sign in book. If a parent drops her child off early in the morning before the child's teacher gets there—or for some reason cannot see the teacher, the director, or some other professional staff member—a message in the notebook is the signal for the teacher to contact the parent. This device recognizes that many parents cannot telephone the school from their jobs during the day and tries to take measures to close that gap. It's not foolproof, but it's another way of reaching out.

The newsletter Ann Chin referred to is the so-called *Friday Letter*, a weekly one-page newsletter, written by a teacher in each class, informing parents about the little things that happened in the class during the week, the new things the kids learned, the games they played, the books they read, and the things they talked about. And parents call on the phone all the time. Usually, they're put right through to the classroom and talk to the teacher directly. The teacher will be asked on the intercom if she can talk to a parent at that moment. If she can't because she is in the middle of some activity with her class, the school will arrange for her to call the parent back. Individual conferences between parents and teacher are scheduled twice a year on a staggered basis. This gives parents and teachers the chance to discuss the child in a more comprehensive way. More parent-teacher conferences are held if either wants it.

An interesting point Jeannine makes is that when the teacher writes up the reports on parent-teacher conferences, she wants to know first what the parent shared with the teacher about the child or the home or what concerns they had. Her aim is to start with the parent, not with the teacher. "We don't want the teacher simply to report that the child can recognize ten letters or she can add, or she's reading or she's a problem and can't get along with people. We start with the parent. We get the parent talking first. And then, from there you can fill in with what you've observed and then how you've observed and then how you can work together on the kinds of things that concern the parent and you."

You're Not Listening!

Early one morning the following scene was observed by a Rosa Lee Young staff member:

A prekindergarten child, who had just turned 3 years old, was being dropped off at school one morning by her father and an older brother. The family was coming down the stairs after hanging up the child's coat. The little girl was asking her father a question, but her father and brother were talking to each other and did not hear her. She asked the same question twice more and still her father did not respond.

As the little girl reached the next to last step, she firmly placed her hands on her hips, looked very upset, and in a loud voice said, "Clearly, you are not listening to my words."

Her father stopped in his tracks and looked at his daughter quite surprised and then gave her his undivided attention. As he passed the staff member in the hallway, he shrugged his shoulders in disbelief. The school official explained that the teachers encourage the children to be respectful and to listen to each other's words.

Dad smiled and replied, "Next time, I'll pay more attention."

A parents' group was formed that meets regularly. The group invites guest speakers, authorities in the field of child care to speak and answer questions. Events include a welcoming Back to School night in the fall; a picnic in the spring for children, their parents, and their teachers; and other activities that bring family and school together. The school director attends these meetings, which provides an opportunity for engagement and discussion with parents. She is also on the committee that plans meetings and events.

Such extensive communication is vital because no program for young children, no matter how good, can ever be completely successful unless the parents and the community understand what the school is doing and unless parents have an input into the process.

Relationship With Parents Must Be a Relationship Among Equals

It's often very easy to criticize parents. Anyone who's ever raised a child has always been aware of the old cliché, "We all make mistakes." How many of us from time to time have looked back at an incident in our own parenting experience and said, "I should have handled that one differently." It's very easy for someone looking on from the outside, particularly a child care professional, to take a harsh and critical approach toward some parents of the children in their care.

Yes, of course, sometimes they are right. There are parents who have such problems of their own that their relationships with their children are destructive ones. Some parents are physically abusive. Others can belittle their children or demean them or otherwise not build the kind of confidence they need to

---

We're Safe in Here

In the family corner of one class, Freddie and Robert are playing at making soup in a plastic pot.

Robert: It's really, really hot. A monster is going to get soup.

Jamie: No monster here in school.

---

explore and to learn. The old adage, "For every problem child there is a problem parent," more often than not rings true.

But most parents love their children and are totally committed to their welfare. And they want to do the right thing at all times. That's why it's so essential for the child care center to have a close relationship with the parents of the children they see every day. And that relationship must be a relationship among equals, not one where the parent looks down at the child care provider as just a babysitter who can be told what to do. Or not one in which the child care professional adopts an attitude of "we've had courses on children so we know all about them and we'll tell you how to raise your child." Alice Honig reported on interviews with family child care providers, one of whom warned, "It's easy for caregivers to fall into the trap of feeling that they are doing everything right and that parents are doing everything wrong."[57]

Indeed, as Honig observed: "The relationship between provider and parent affects the child's attachment to both. A supportive parent-caregiver relationship strengthens the child's attachment to the caregiver and his comfort in the setting, as he picks up the message that his mother values this person and trusts her to take care of him. Caregivers likewise should communicate their respect for the parents. Children's major resources are their parents, and providers and teachers should convey to parents how deeply important they are in helping their children thrive. Many parents are stressed; they may be worried about money, health, jobs, or personal relationships. They appreciate the caregiver's affirming how very special they are to their child." Or as a family child care provider interviewed by Honig cautioned, "Parent-provider relationships make or break the business. . . . You have to bend and be flexible. You can't be cut-and-dried in your judgments." Another says, "It is important to set limits for yourself by respecting parents as heads of their own household."[58]

The lesson here is a vital one for any successful early child care program: A relationship of mutual respect and cooperation between parents and the child care center and its professional staff is essential for the program to work.

Or, as an article in one leading periodical in the profession summarized it: "Parenting advice is not nearly as important to families as other forms of communication that pertain more directly to the child's social and emotional development and performance in school. Parents regard advice giving as intrusive.

They prefer cooperative, respectful communication within the context of reciprocal relationships. Without such relationships, parents can be reluctant to talk to teachers." What this means for early childhood educators, says the article's authors, is that the early childhood center must offer regular and frequent communication about the child and should reach out and communicate to all families about what they can expect from the program and the teachers."[59]

But What If a Parent's Behavior Is Harmful to the Child?

But what if the school does observe parental behavior that is abusive or what it feels is clearly harmful to the child and completely contrary to its childrearing philosophy? In some countries, for example, corporal punishment is still used in the schools—although it is on the decline throughout the world—and some parents who come from those countries are often disappointed when the school frowns upon it.

Famed child psychologist Alicia F. Lieberman, director of the Infant-Parent program at the University of California, San Francisco, gives an example of how this problem was handled at her center. Instead of meeting the problem head on and telling the parent that corporal punishment is wrong, the center took a different approach. Rather than "trying to change the attitudes we did not like, we concentrated on trying to understand the mother's feelings towards her child and her perception of what was good for the child," Lieberman wrote. In one case a mother spoke about how disobedient her 15-month-old son was and how she had begun to spank him to change his behavior.

> We first empathized with how difficult it was when the child got into everything, particularly since the whole family lived in one small room and it was hard enough to keep things tidy after a long day at work. Then very slowly, as the mother spoke about how hard things were for the family in such tight quarters, we sympathetically linked the difficult conditions with the mother's short fuse towards her son. She was receptive to this, and then we moved one step further and commented lightly that when one is stressed out it is easy to forget that at 15 months children have a lot of energy and a very short memory. The mother laughed and said, in a sad tone, that it was easy to use children as scapegoats. This led to a discussion of children's feelings, and memories about how she was disciplined with a belt. I asked her if she respected her parents when they did that. She said yes, but she was also scared of them. I asked her if she thought that fear and respect went together. She smiled and said: "Sometimes." After a silence, she said thoughtfully that she never felt close to her parents, and that she didn't want her son to be scared of her. This opened the door to a recurrent discussion of how best to instill respect in children, and children's natural wish to please their parents as a basic psychological underpinning for obedience and respect.

Lieberman cited this as an example of how child care center administrators, social workers, and psychologists can use the parents' own feelings and experience "to promote more responsiveness to the child's developmental and emotional needs as we can see them." She concludes that learning to see the world as parents see it, at least while we are with them, is important in understanding problems in the behavior of parents toward their children and taking steps to correct it.[60]

Of course, it cannot always work out this way. Teachers and administrators are not all psychologists, and the parents who engage in harmful behavior toward their children often have problems that go well beyond the intervention process described previously. But the basic principle of reciprocal relationships between parents and teachers as a means of keeping open cooperative, respectful communication between them is at the heart of a good early child care program.

Getting the School's Message Across

Communication with parents is important, not only for the welfare of the child but also to inform parents of what the school is doing and help them understand the program and aims of the child care center. In these times when so much stress is being placed upon teaching children academics beginning with the earliest age groups, there is great fear among some child care educators that parents will not understand a developmentally appropriate approach and will demand that the school teach their children reading, math, and science. "The best way to address parents' concerns is through ongoing communication," counseled two experienced figures in the field. "The more often teachers communicate with families about what children are doing and learning in their classroom, the more likely a family is to understand the value of a developmentally appropriate approach. . . . Most parents want what is best for their child, and the majority of their questions and concerns can be addressed by providing information, inviting their involvement and helping to empower them." By showing parents how they are actually getting children to engage in "independent thinking and academic and social problem solving," they wrote, families are able to understand "that implementing developmentally appropriate practices does not mean decreasing the amount of academic rigor in your classroom or neglecting to teach math, reading, science, or other important subjects. The better you communicate that this approach to curriculum development is based on research and knowledge of child development the more likely families are to support your efforts."[61]

It doesn't work perfectly. Getting working parents involved in a school is always a difficult job because there are so many other factors that stand in the way. But administrators and teachers are constantly trying. And the degree to which they have been able to involve parents is the direct result of their efforts.

The involvement of parents in building an understanding of the real aim of early childhood education was underlined for me by a parent, Nicola Farman, whose daughter attended Rosa Lee Young for more than five years after some very negative experiences with other centers. "The whole feel of Rosa Lee Young as a childhood center is much more relaxed, much more child focused," she said emphatically. "The philosophy of Rosa Lee Young is that learning is about exploring, not about shoving useless memorization of facts into your head. And the love of learning, which I believe is instilled by the teaching methodology at Rosa Lee Young, is completely counter to what happens at many other centers and in many kindergarten classes.

"I'll give you an example. My child was here in the toddler class for just a short time when one evening at home we were talking. I had a set of alphabet letters that stick on the side of a refrigerator and I was amazed that my child identified every letter. When I came into the school the next day, I told her teacher and said I thought it was amazing. And the teacher looked at me and said, 'That's good, but you know, I don't teach them to memorize. I teach how to learn, how to solve a problem.' And I said, 'That's it! That's exactly what one needs to know. Memorization will come. But the innate desire to learn can be squashed like a bug. I don't want that.'"

How Does Your Child Care Center Build Relationships Between Caregiver, Child, and Family?

1. Do the child care center staff members respond warmly to children who need their attention? Do they speak softly and lovingly to each individual child? Do they frequently hug the children?

2. Do teachers get down on the floor when they play with the children so they can be close to each of them at their level?

3. Is the school's schedule flexible enough to allow for special problems that sometimes arise from individual children?

4. Are the special strengths of some children—good at athletics, reading, games, and so on—used to enrich the class and build the ego of the individual child? Is the teacher aware of each child's unique personality so she can understand and work with the child's individual needs?

5. Are the children's feelings of empathy encouraged by the example of the teacher's showing empathy with the problems of individual children?

6. Are classroom chores shared among the children so they develop a sense of responsibility for the entire group?

7. Does the school strive to create a link between the families and the class via pictures on the bulletin boards of the children's families and other devices, encouraging children to talk about their homes and families? Are families welcomed into

(Continued)

(Continued)

the school? Is there ongoing communication between the parent and the school? Does the school know all about the child from information continually provided by the parent so they can better understand the child's individual needs?

8. Is the school's relationship with the parents based on mutual equality and respect so that neither gets the feeling of being "spoken down to"?

9. Does the school employ a full-time social worker who is available for children with special problems? In the case of special children, such as those with physical or speech problems, are outside services like occupational or speech therapists available to come into the school?

10. When the school feels that a parent's behavior is harmful to the child, is it handled in a way that will help the parent see the problem? If there is real harmful behavior on the part of the parent or if the child has special needs that cannot be handled by the school, does the school have contact with outside agencies and authorities who can be helpful?

The Second Task

Developing Wholesome Peer Relationships Among Children

Children treat their friends differently than they treat the other people in their lives. A friendship is a place for experimenting with new ways of handling anger and aggression. It is an arena for practicing reciprocity, testing assertiveness, and searching for compromise in ways children would not try with parents or siblings.

—Lawrence Kutner

We all work together with a wiggle and a giggle,
We all work together with a giggle and a grin.

—Woody Guthrie

The building of healthy relationships among the children is one of the prime tasks of a good early child care program. This chapter explains why this is so. It then illustrates

- How the daily class activities teach children to cooperate and share ideas on daily tasks and play projects
- How children are encouraged by their teachers to resolve conflicts that arise among them in a way that engenders self-respect and confidence

This chapter also discusses in detail and provides examples, through the interaction of the children in the classroom, of the stages of play that children go through, illustrating

- How opportunities for peer interaction are created at different stages of play
- How building blocks for successful interpersonal relationships later on are developed at each stage of play
- How relationships among the children and peer play can be used by teachers to develop creative thinking in the children

It was about halfway through the morning in the prekindergarten and kindergarten class of Lisa Streb and Sally Ann Braman. After Lisa had described the activities in the different areas of the room, the children chose where they wanted to go. They then formed into groups and busily worked in the separate areas. In one section two children were looking at some games on a computer and discussing them. In a second area Sally and three children were playing a modified version of Bingo in which each child in turn had to think of a word. The other children then raised their hands to tell what letter the word started with, and the children then placed small disks over that letter on the individual cards in front of them until one child filled up a straight row of letters on his card. In another area Danielle and Isabelle were pretending to diaper babies at a table and talking to each other about babies "pooping" and being diapered. In still another area, three boys—Richard, Gilbert, and Joey—were playing with Legos and small doll-like figures, using them to construct fire engines and rescue people. Joey particularly liked to play at the fire engine game. His father is a New York City firefighter who once visited the school and spoke to the children in his son's class about the work that firefighters do while Joey sat there smiling proudly from ear to ear. As they played at their "rescue people" game, Richard became frustrated at something and didn't like the way the other two treated him, so he went to Sally and complained. Lisa was busy with some other children at the time, so Sally left the Bingo game, took Richard back to the group, and sat on the floor and joined the three boys in their game. She didn't admonish anybody or even say anything about the little dispute. She just joined in with them, prompting Richard to join, too, by directing some tasks at him. After a while, in an action that naturally flowed from the situation, the other two included Richard and the four of them played at firefighting. Sally's presence made Richard more secure and made them able to accept him, particularly as he began to make positive contributions to the group.

Meanwhile back at the Bingo game, something very interesting was occurring. Before Sally left, one of the boys, Peter, had come up with an idea for a different version of the game. His idea was that each child, instead of saying a word, would say a letter, and the other children would think of a word that began with that letter. They would then follow the game as before, placing a disk over the initial letter on their cards. The others thought it was a good idea, and the game resumed with the new modification. Peter looked proud of himself and quickly assumed the role of leader of the group. When the teacher had to go over to handle the other situation with Richard, she quietly told them that Richard needed her help and they were to go on playing while she was away. Peter, sympathetically observing that Richard was upset and encouraged by Sally's instruction that the children carry on, just naturally moved in and took charge of the Bingo game, and the rest of the group cooperated to help their teacher and their classmate.

All these cases serve to illustrate one of the most important functions of a quality early child care program: encouraging the development of wholesome peer relationships among children.

WHY BUILDING PEER RELATIONSHIPS IS A NECESSITY AMONG CHILDREN

Adults know that relationships among friends are important, often a source of joy. They are fundamental to us as human beings. When studying the actions of children, we follow a tendency to concentrate solely on the parent-child bond or the relationships between teachers and children. Even though these are fundamental, the relationship of a child to other children is also vital for the development of young children. These peer relationships serve to foster several necessary steps in the growth of the individual child.

First, they build self-esteem in the child. All children want to be liked by their peers—it is a natural stage in human development. As they play with other children, they contribute to the play situation and are accepted as a natural part of it. It makes them feel good when their ideas are accepted by others and become part of the script for the group. Witness what happened with Peter.

Second, they help them to learn how to negotiate situations with others. In the real world, no one is an island. We are all interdependent upon others in every aspect of our daily lives. Life, therefore, is a constant process of negotiation and accommodation with other people, and this process begins in childhood.

Third, they help children to learn social and emotional skills that are absolutely necessary in human relationships. They learn to read the emotions of others—when they are happy or sad, when they want to do some particular thing and when they don't.

"Establishing relationships with other children is one of the major developmental tasks of early childhood," according to the definitive study *From Neurons to Neighborhoods*.

How well children fare at this task appears to matter. It matters to the children themselves, creating a context in which they evaluate their self-worth, competence, and view of the world as pleasant or hostile. It matters to their future, as the patterns of peer interaction in early childhood increasingly predict whether children will walk pathways to competence or deviance in the tasks of middle childhood and adolescence. And it matters to the other children a child comes into contact with, as the experience of children in peer groups depends in good measure on the nature of the other children with whom they interact.[62]

Or, as another prominent researcher, put it:

While adults remain central to the child's feeling of well-being at this age, peers are also compelling, and relationships with other people are growing in significance. Children are motivated to negotiate with one another over toys and shared space in order to have the pleasure of each other's company. As the negotiations proceed and the socialization process unfolds, there is less struggle over issues of domain and more energy can be devoted to the emergence of dramatic play skills. Children begin to pool their symbols and their play metaphors and to create collaborative play ventures that allow a more profound level of sharing to occur. Not only can children share materials, but they can share experiences with one another through play. This important avenue allows them to diminish feelings of isolation and to feel empowered in a miniature world of their own design.[63]

The author recommended frequent open-ended play periods during the course of the day in child care centers because that is where "children are encouraged to focus on and interpret naturally occurring affective events. These opportunities give children experience in reading affect messages from peers within the classroom milieu, where teachers can help them interpret messages and provide protection from emotional content that may be overwhelming.[64]

Indeed, if we examine the play activities in that one short space of time in that one class, we will see just how much children are gaining in their lives, both socially and cognitively, through the application of solid principles of child care in a good preschool setting.

THE STAGES OF PLAY

Much of what we know today about the central role of play in the development and learning processes of children is derived from the pioneering work of Lev Vygotsky and those who elaborated on his work. The Vygotskian approach emphasized the cognitive connections between play and literacy at various stages in the child's development.

Watching Closely: The Onlooker Stage of Play

Peer play doesn't mean the child is always engaged in active play. Some children go through a stage in which they are totally engrossed in the play of others by simply watching them and being caught up in their experiences without actually participating. In the November 2002 issue of *Young Children, The Journal of the National Association for the Education of Young Children,* Sarah Jane Anderson, Associate Professor of Early Childhood Education at Mount Ida College in Massachusetts, described the onlooker stage of play in which the child participates passively in the play of other children.

She described a preschooler named Jack who "immediately engages in the play of others" upon entering the room in his class. He actively follows "the towering building being constructed in the block center, the battle of the dinosaurs in the sandbox, the jumping and twisting in the gross motor area, the puppet show just started in the dramatic play corner." He would smile "at the antics of the children pretending to be monkeys and gorillas, and his whole body would become rigid and tense as two children collided in the jumping area." In this onlooker stage, the author wrote, "Jack is fully engaged—without moving one step away from his cubby."

This onlooker stage gives some children the opportunity to mentally engage with other children and learn from their actions without the "potential intimidation" of being in the middle of things. It allows them to organize and integrate the experience in their minds and store it away for some future time. Parents and preschool teachers are often anxious, said the writer, if preschoolers do not participate in overt play with other children. "Perhaps we should allow them more time," she said, "to watch and learn; when the time is right, they will be more comfortable and successful stepping into the world of full social interaction."

Let's start with the two girls playing at diapering the imaginary baby. Their entire activity involves what child care professionals call *symbolic play,* or *pretend play,* which is the highest form of play in the early childhood years. A brief observation of play development in the earliest years clearly confirms this. At first, the newborn is interested only in its mother who provides it with food, comfort, and his only contact with the outside world. But research has shown that as early as 2 months, "young infants get excited by the sight of other infants and, when given the opportunity, they will stare avidly at one another." The pattern of growth progresses to babies smiling and babbling at other babies at 6 to 9 months to the beginning of interaction with each other between 1 to 2 years.[65]

Imitation, the First Form of Interaction

Until recently it was believed that this interaction between two children under the age of 2 was only what was called *parallel play,* that is, children playing side by side, comforted by each other but not really playing with each other.

More recent research, however, has established that there is far more of an interchange between playmates at this age than was previously thought. The interaction often takes the form of imitation where one child follows the lead of another child, copying his activities, with the children often taking turns at imitating each other. Remember the toddlers in Pepper Robinson's class described in Chapter 1? They were engaged in various forms of copying. When the two children played at the water table, one child poured water in a cup and then spilled it out and the other child repeated the same action afterward. Their play together consisted of watching each other fill the cup and spilling out the water, essentially imitating each other. Even their conversation at the breakfast table was to pick up on something another said and imitate it with perhaps some variation in fact or fantasy rather than truly responding to it. Recall one girl's reporting that her mommy has a baby in her tummy and a boy replying that he too has a baby in his tummy.

Reciprocal Symbolic Interactive Play

This evolves around the age of 2 and continues to 3 and beyond. Here, children begin to become aware of what other children are doing and react to them. This interactive play gradually becomes more and more complex. With adult guidance this is when children can learn to take turns at an activity, become aware of the intent of other children, take on reciprocal roles, and begin to engage in coordinated play with rules. After a while, the child's imagination becomes part of his regular play routine.

"As children move into the preschool years, their social skills expand dramatically. Play among preschoolers increasingly involves pretense, and pretense increasingly includes playing with things that don't depend on the props available. By age 5, most children can quickly set up elaborate pretend play, making almost anything stand for almost anything else. The number of children who can be included in play at one time also expands, [until, by age 5, children can often play with three or more at a time] keeping track of what roles all are playing, how their roles fit in the overall theme, and negotiating conflicts to decide together what is and what isn't supposed to happen next."[66]

In the class the two girls Danielle and Isabelle were engaged in an elaborate activity of pretend play. They diapered imaginary dolls, going through the motions with their hands, pretending the babies were in front of them having their diapers changed. They discussed how these "babies" pooped and had to be cleaned. They took turns diapering each other's "baby," discussing, disagreeing, and finally agreeing to a procedure they both followed. After a while, Joey came over from his Legos area and played with the girls. "Help me," he said to them. "You need to help me with the baby. He pooped." I don't know if they were trying to counter a gender stereotype or if it was simply a coincidental remark but one of the girls responded, "My daddy changes the baby's diaper."

Whereas most adults would not think much about it except to feel how cute it is, these three children were involved in an advanced form of play that was teaching them a great deal. They were learning to use their imaginations, to recall past scenes with which they were familiar, repeating them and elaborating on them. They were using language to describe and communicate with each other what they were doing and to negotiate differences. And they were establishing rules and procedures for a task that they followed. Taken together, their peer activity was sharpening both the social and cognitive skills that will be an important building block for their development in both areas.

The teacher in these cases does not discourage symbolic play, unless of course it could hurt the child or others (such as if the child wanted to pretend to be Superman and fly out of a window, although nearly all children instinctively know the limits to how far their pretend play can go). On the contrary, the trained early childhood teacher encourages pretend play, usually by joining in the game, or at least in the pretense. You could see the extent of the encouragement of symbolic play by the way children in every class at Rosa Lee Young engaged in it. Every class, as I've noted, has a time period when children are encouraged to seek play activities on their own in one of the separate areas of the room, and the children will inevitably drift into pretend games. In Linda Schnitzer's class, I observed Carson join Robert and Molly at the playdough table making "pizza" and "hot dogs" and tasting it. "Yum, yum," said Carson, smacking his lips after pretending to bite into the morsels, "mustard."

In Barbara Quinterno's class, two boys, Joseph and Richard, were so engrossed in something they were building in the block area they didn't even notice me listening in to their intensive conversation. What is it they were building? Why, a skyrocket, of course. Anybody could see that!

Children make up a story as the teacher writes it in a class book.

In another class the teacher put some soap into the water at the water table and stirred it into a sudsy mixture for the two children who were playing there with plastic animals and sponges. They were both busy washing toy dinosaurs and engaging in a lengthy discourse about their project. Ethan began the conversation.

Ethan: I sponge you up. You are all dirty.

Jack (a child not too sure of himself): Me?

Ethan: No, this dinosaur.

Jack: What's your favorite color?

Ethan: My birdie's dirty. I have to wash my birdie all up.

Jack (to teacher as he scrubs dinosaur with sponge): Hi, Sally. Look, Sally.

Teacher: Do a good job.

Jack: I'm getting them clean.

Ethan: Stop copying my words.

Teacher: He likes your words. That's why he's using them.

Ethan: They are my dinosaurs.

Angela (as she comes over to them): Are you using these?

Jack: I'll give you one.

Ethan: I want to work by myself. (He takes a dinosaur from Jack.)

Jack: I'm not going to be your friend.

(Angela joins them.)

Angela: These are my dinosaurs. This is a mommy dinosaur. That's a daddy. That's a baby.

Ethan (to a small dinosaur): Did someone draw on you?

(Angela puts soap on sponges and helps them clean.)

Ethan (a little annoyed by her attempt to help him): I'm fine. I'm fine. (Then moving the dinosaur through the air as if it is flying): I'm flying, Daddy. Help me.

Jack (imitates Ethan): My dinosaurs can fly.

Ethan (in a falsetto voice speaking for the dinosaur): I want Daddy. I want Daddy.

Angela: Come, I'll help you. I can fly.

(Jack now plays by himself, scrubbing and cleaning his dinosaur.)

Ethan: I'm finished.

Angela: I'm finished.

When teachers join in the pretense, they can stimulate the child to think further with questions that challenge her about the situation she has created. Take for example, the exchange among three children and the teacher in a prekindergarten class at Rosa Lee Young that I observed one day. A girl, Holly, and a boy, Freddie, were playing in the family corner. The following dialogue ensued:

Holly: Freddie, where's my pocketbook?

Freddie (talking excitedly into a toy telephone): Baby is very sick.

Holly: Freddie, we have to sit down. (Freddie tries to sit down.) No, Freddie, you're sitting on my baby. (She picks up her doll.) We're getting ready to go to the zoo with baby. We're going to see alligators, big tigers. We're going to see pumas, little baby pumas. We're going to see little baby pumas.

Freddie: I'm not going.

(They look at each other in a wall mirror in the family corner. He takes a pocketbook from a table where she placed it and puts it on his arm. She takes a necktie from a basket in the family corner and puts it on him. She also takes a "princess dress" and a fur collar from the basket and puts them on and repeats)

Holly: We're going to the zoo.

Freddie: You're a princess. We let you be a princess every day.

Holly (pointing to an open zipper on the back of her "princess dress" as she turns around and bends over): Can you help me zipper up my dress? (Freddie works on the zipper until he zippers it up. Then they make believe he has a camera and he takes a picture of her.)

(The teacher now joins in on the conversation.)

Teacher (to Freddie): You look so handsome in your tie.

At this point the dialogue ended and the children drifted off to play at something else.

The teacher here missed a rich opportunity to probe the imaginations of the children with questions like

- Freddie, are you a daddy?
- It looks like you're going away. Where are you going?
- (If they say "to the zoo") You're going to see pumas and alligators and tigers. What other animals will you see?

- What do animals do at the zoo?
- Are you taking your baby to the zoo?
- (If they say "no") Why?

Simple *why, what, where, when, and how* questions should be used with children to attempt to elicit imaginative responses. As the professional journal *Young Children* pointed out, "Learning and creativity grow when situations pique children's interest and stretch their imaginations. . . . Free-choice time (when children choose their activities) is an opportunity for teachers to talk with individuals or small groups of children about their chosen activities. An engaged adult can help children build on and extend their learning by first observing what the children are doing and saying and then offering specific comments or questions to extend children's thinking and vocabulary."[67]

Engaging in Games With Rules

Or take the Bingo game, a nonsymbolic activity, that another group was playing with words and letters instead of numbers. The game clearly involved engaging in an activity with rules. Who goes next, what letter is correct as the start of a word, how a game progresses, and all the rest. It even involves handling the concept that some child's card will fill up first and he may be the winner, possibly causing some others to feel inadequate or frustrated, which requires skill on the part of the teacher in anticipating and avoiding any hurt feelings that may arise. Children thus can learn to lose a game without losing self-esteem. And, of course, this group game, played among peers, strongly sharpened the cognitive skill of recognizing words and letters, a major step toward learning to read.

Using Play to Encourage Creative Thinking

But two other things happened during the Bingo game that illustrate crucial points in the development of healthy peer relationships among young children. By coming up with a different version of the game, Peter was thinking creatively. When the others thought his idea was a good one, it not only built his ego but also helped to teach the children to listen to each other's ideas and to constructively engage with each other. And when the teacher had to leave the group for a few moments to attend to Richard, the group's empathy with their frustrated classmate in this situation led them to cooperate with the teacher and go on with the game.

Children express their own experiences through play, and beginning from about the age of 2, if they are encouraged, they always elaborate on them creatively. In a child care classroom, the teacher can set the stage and encourage the children with questions, but the children themselves, through their play, will come up with the most novel ideas. Their brains are constantly working, conjuring up new images, many of them silly to adults but quite logical to the children. If the play is not discouraged, it develops the imaginations and their

A Bit of Creativity in One Child's Play

In the family corner where the children are playing doctor, one child is pretending to iron an imaginary shirt with a toy plastic iron.

Girl: I'm making believe I'm ironing.

Teacher: But we're doctors today.

Girl: I'm ironing my doctor's shirt.

creativity and is a wonderful step on the way to their development as thinking human beings.

Take for example a situation at Rosa Lee Young: Several classes took a trip to a local hospital in which there was a special room, a "teddy bear clinic" for children. They were shown what X-rays are, how casts are applied to broken bones, how people get oxygen, and how stitches are applied to bad wounds. The children brought stuffed animals to this "clinic" to be "made better." Back at the school, the children had small white doctor's coats, surgical masks, and surgical caps for play.

A day after the visit, two children in the prekindergarten class, Lamont and Craig, were playing in the family corner.

Lamont (takes doctor's coat and says to teacher): Help me put this on. (She helps him to put on the coat and the plastic surgical cap.)

Lamont (to Craig): Can you hold this baby for a minute?

Lamont (puts stethoscope on his ears and holds end up to Craig's chest): I'm going to check your heart.

Craig: Boom, boom.

Lamont: Here's some medicine.

Craig: I don't have a boo boo.

(Lamont gently gives injection to doll.)

Craig: I'm making purple tea with stuffing.

Lamont: I'm making some orange tea.

Craig: That's great.

In the kindergarten class in another room, two children were also playing doctor in the family corner. They put on surgical masks and blue surgeon's shirts.

David (to a doll): I'll give you a shot. (Then referring to the teacher): She needs a shot.

Joshua (goes over to teacher): Do you want a shot? (Teacher sits on chair and gets a shot from Joshua while David holds a toy stethoscope to her back.) I want to examine your lungs.

Teacher: Am I healthy?

David: We forgot to check your ears. (They check her ears.)

(The two boys then have a little dispute over a blanket that each of them wants.)

David (to Joshua): You don't seem happy.

Joshua: Because I want to use it for the baby. (Then he pauses and reconsiders.) I'll use it when you're done.

David: Help me put my mask on. (Joshua helps him.) Thank you.

Joshua: You're welcome. (They then proceed to help each other put on surgical caps and masks.)

(A girl, Lisa, observing their play at doctor, comes over to them with a doll.)

Lisa: I have to fix the baby. Her heart is breathing.

David: I want the blanket because my baby is sick.

Joshua: Can we share the blanket?

David: Yes.

Joshua (to teacher): Can you watch us play?

Teacher: I'm watching.

The children at play here are engaging in all sorts of imaginative variations on the doctor scene, like the baby whose "heart is breathing" and making "purple tea with stuffing" in the midst of their doctoring. The teacher can help the situation by asking probing questions, allowing them time to think and respond about what they're playing, without stifling their creative fantasies. Or the teacher can offer suggestions for extending play, staying within the play theme. As Greenspan noted, "All kinds of situations, from dialogues about games, meals, trips, even bedtime, encourage both logic and fantasy. Dialogues with children who are asking the 'W' questions (Who, What, When, Where, Why) encourage them to express their wishes, think about connections, and come up with new ideas. When these ideas are not nipped in the bud, a child's mind and imagination expand and his confidence in his own ability to communicate ideas grows."[68]

A major goal of a good early child care environment is to actively encourage and build healthy relationships among peers. "Growth in peer interaction is dramatic across the first several years of life," noted one study. "Cooperation, negotiation, and leadership are learned during early interactions with same-age peers."

Children's relations with their peers, the study's authors pointed out, "are important for a number of reasons. Peers influence children's social, cognitive, and emotional development. Interaction with peers provides an individual child with the opportunities to learn effective communication skills, to learn to control his or her aggressive behavior and to learn cooperative interpersonal skills. . . . Peers provide a child with a sounding board for his or her ideas, a 'mirror level' of cognitive sophistication against which the child can evaluate and test out ideas, and opportunities for mutual exchange that are not possible in interaction with a parent or other adult. The peer group context also has been cited as providing a secure base for emotional expression. . . . Peers provide social support and contribute to the development and concept of self. The nature of a child's relationship with his or her agemates thus may have an enormous impact on his or her adjustment and development."[69]

TEACHING CHILDREN TO RESOLVE CONFLICTS: AN ESSENTIAL TASK OF EARLY CHILDHOOD EDUCATORS

The group activity involving Legos construction of fire engines and play at rescuing people presented a problem that is inevitable in this age group and a challenge to the skilled teacher in handling it: conflict among children and its resolution *in a way that teaches them how to resolve such conflicts*. "Toddler play and friendships, of course, are not all sunshine and light," child care authorities concede. "Conflict happens. Indeed, conflict and aggression initially increase as children try to play together, peaking between years 2 and 3 before they decline. It may come as some relief to parents that in the toddler and early preschool period, moderately aggressive children are often the most socially outgoing." But while "conflict of the 'beat 'em up, drag 'em down' variety is not good for anyone," these authorities say, learning how to resolve conflicts is extremely important to the child's development. When it occurs, they can "walk away, slug it out, give in, argue and negotiate, or appeal to higher powers." But friends "are more likely to stick it out, negotiate, compromise, and continue to play," a big step toward "competent social behavior."[70] The teaching of conflict resolution at a young age is, therefore, an important part of the job of early childhood educators.

In the Legos group as noted, Richard became upset with something and walked away to complain to the teacher. Now, there are several ways the teacher could have handled the situation. She could have gotten upset with the children for causing a problem for Richard, or she could have gone over and forcefully made sure Richard was included in the game. But her approach was that these are very young children, they are in the process of learning how to resolve conflicts, and her task was to help them learn. She simply went to the group with Richard, sat on the floor, and joined the group in play along with Richard. With both the teacher and Richard sitting there and participating as if nothing had happened, the children just naturally went on with the game and Richard became a part of it.

Valentine's Day. The class made get well valentines for patients at a local hospital.

In fact, teachers of very young children are most often involved in the resolution of conflicts and must always keep one cardinal rule in mind: Hostile behavior of one child toward another cannot be handled in the same way it is done in the case of older children. Of course, it should be dealt with so that the child knows this is not the way to behave, but always without shaming the child or making him feel less of a person.

Take an occurrence I witnessed in Linda Schnitzer's class. Two boys, Robert and Carson, were playing at the computer when suddenly a row erupted, and Robert became very upset. Carson had spit in his face. Linda came over and held both children around. "Where did he spit?" she asked Robert, who touched a spot on his face. She then looked into Carson's eyes and said to him, "You must really be angry to spit at Robert. But we must never do that. If we're angry, we use words. Do you think you can do that?" The little boy nodded.

After a short time, she left them alone together and watched them as they resumed their computer game and then went together to another activity. By showing affection to both of them, the teacher was telling each child that she cared about him. That was the most important thing in this situation. Even as she was telling one child that his behavior was not appropriate, she was making them both feel respected and more emotionally receptive to what she was saying. Of course, this doesn't mean that Carson won't do it again sometime. What occurred was part of his learning process, and any learning process needs constant reinforcement. It's just one step along the way.

As Brazelton and Greenspan summed it up in more academic terms: "Time with friends is a very important developmental experience for preschoolers. . . . Peer play helps a child's learning about relationships and involves advanced reflective skills to negotiate the complexities that come up in peer relationships."[71] Or, in the words of another child psychologist, "The development of these positive relationships among peers, gives the child opportunities for communication, reality testing, forming relationships, gaining insight, sublimation, attaining mastery, and stimulating symbolic activity."[72]

It is instructive to watch Linda and her coteacher, Vanessa Weiss-Barkofsky, as they constantly play the role of arbitrator when differences arise among the children. Making them aware of how to negotiate with one another, they consistently say such things as, "What can you do? Should you yell at him? That's not good. Let's try something else." Or, "We don't hurt our friends." In fact, the word *friend* is probably the most used word in their vocabularies. Rarely do they say a child's name to another child without prefixing it with the word. "Your friend, Robert, is in the corner." Or, "How shall you and your friend, Helena, solve this problem?" It's all priority instruction in a good early child care program—teaching children how to work with their peers.

The Conversationalist

An early morning conversation in the toddler classroom:

Sally (2 years, 5 months old): You love your daddy, Roger?

Roger (2 years, 8 months old): Yeah.

Sally: He's a nice man, Roger.

Roger: I like cars.

Sally: Roger, can you press this button on the book?

Roger: Why are you talking a lot to me, Sally?

Sally: I like reading books. This says "Beep. Beep."

Roger: I don't want to talk. I want to build.

That's, of course, the rub: a *good* early child care program. In the Introduction we reported the results of a study that found only 14 percent of child care for all age groups adequate, with the percentage of adequate care even lower for infants and toddlers, and another long-term specialist in the field declaring that, as of the mid-1990s, only 10 percent of the day care centers in the United States could be considered good and that 40 percent actually did harm to the children. In child care which does not hire highly competent staff, the interactions I have described in this chapter can lead to destructive results instead of helping children to grow.

From Neurons to Neighborhoods noted some "contradictory findings" in a number of studies of early child care for infants and toddlers in the first two years of life. "On one hand, preschool children with prior experience with peers in child care have been found to be more involved, positive, and cooperative with peers than preschoolers without such experience and to engage in more complex forms of play. This is especially the case when children remain with the same group of peers over time." However, it notes, "On the other hand, extensive child care in the first two years of life has been associated with lower social competence and heightened aggression in preschool and beyond. The clue to these contradictory findings seems to lie in the quality of care that is provided and, in particular, in the sensitivity of the relationships that caregivers establish with their young charges. Higher-quality child care is generally related to more competent peer relationships during early childhood and into the school years."[73]

And so, we end this chapter on a similar note to the way we ended others in this book—by citing our own experience at the center. Just going in, looking at the classes, seeing these professionals working with children, and then seeing the results in the children themselves, tells the whole story. For those of us who have dedicated ourselves to the welfare of children, it is a story that makes us feel that whatever other problems there are in this field, there is still plenty of room for optimism.

What Steps Does Your Child Care Center Take to Build Positive Relationships Among the Children?

1. Does the child care program encourage children to play among themselves, ever mindful of the skills that come through healthy peer relationships?

2. Is the peer play building social skills such as playing cooperatively in a group, taking turns, and accepting each other?

3. Is it building cognitive skills such as children sharing knowledge and experiences with each other?

4. Is it enhancing their emotional growth by encouraging empathetic behavior toward each other; by developing the children's ability to experience and handle aggression, shyness, happiness, sadness; and similar actions?

5. Is the peer play encouraging the building of self-esteem in each child?

6. If the teacher feels the child is doing something inappropriate, does she try to get the child to understand why it is not suitable behavior?

7. Does the program encourage the children to learn how to resolve conflicts by negotiation and compromise rather than by violence? Do teachers know which children are more likely to be aggressive and lose control in a dispute and which can more readily negotiate and compromise? When it is necessary for them to intervene, do they settle disputes among the children in a loving, nonpunitive way without shaming either child in the dispute? Do they ask the children themselves what they think should best be done to solve the problem?

8. Does it encourage creative thinking by allowing children to develop their own variations of the games and activities with each other?

9. Does it encourage exploring different options to solve or engage in a particular activity?

10. Does a child have the freedom to change an activity if he feels the need to? Does a teacher work with a child who has difficulty in focusing on any one activity for a reasonable time at his developmental level?

11. Does the play allow the children to use different sensory stimulation to express themselves through writing, painting, music, construction, or movement?

12. Does the program carefully observe each child to evaluate the developmental stage of play of the child? Do teachers subtly encourage the grouping of children into activities by considering this and the fact that some children may be friends and enjoy being together even if they are at different stages of development?

The Role of Curriculum and Staff Development in Early Child Care

June marks the end of our daughter's learning experience at Rosa Lee Young Childhood Center. She is 5 years old and has attended the center since she was a toddler. She received a wonderful education from a great collection of teachers guided by able administrators. We have no doubt that the vast social and academic skills instilled in her will help her tremendously in kindergarten and beyond.

—Kenneth and Michele Fischgrund,
Letter to the editor of the local paper,
Rockville Centre Herald, June 23, 2005

With a healthy educational philosophy as the most important pillar in the program of a good child care center, we will examine in this chapter two concrete measures that move that philosophy into practical day-to-day work in dealing with children. They are

1. A well-planned, developmentally appropriate curriculum that is not a straitjacket for teachers but serves as a guide to accomplish the educational philosophy of the program and is modified in accord with the interests of the children. This curriculum must include provision for class, small group. and individual activity and must give children the opportunity to choose from a variety of class resources to which children will naturally gravitate that help develop their understanding and skills, both emotionally and cognitively.

2. The continuing process of staff development and inservice training, which is an essential part of professional growth in those who do the everyday work with the children.

THE IMPORTANCE OF A WELL-PLANNED, APPROPRIATE CURRICULUM

We have discussed previously some of the qualities of good early child care: the quality and training of staff; the importance of administrative leadership; the emphasis on developing trust, confidence, and self-esteem in the child's relationship with the adult caregiver and in his cooperative play with other children. And all the time developing his cognitive, emotional, social, and sensory-motor skills. But enunciating a philosophy is just the starting point. What does a child care program do to implement its program? Does it have an overall plan?

In some schools the curriculum strategies today "do not demand enough of children and in other ways demand too much of the wrong thing," according to the National Association for the Education of Young Children. "On the one hand, narrowing the curriculum to those basic skills that can be easily measured on multiple-choice tests diminishes the intellectual challenge for many children. Such an intellectually impoverished curriculum underestimates the true competence of children. . . . On the other hand, curriculum expectations in the early years of schooling sometimes are not appropriate for the age groups served. When next-grade expectations of mastery of basic skills are routinely pushed down to the previous grade level and whole group and teacher-led instruction is the dominant teaching strategy, children who cannot sit still and attend to teacher lectures or who are bored and unchallenged by doing workbook pages for long periods of time are mislabeled as immature, disruptive, or unready for school."[74]

Chapter 6 is devoted to a fuller discussion of this topic. In addition, for an outline of what should determine developmentally appropriate practices at various stages in young children, see the NAEYC Policy Guidelines on this subject in Appendix B.

Keeping this in mind, let's look at the curriculum of Rosa Lee Young. According to its staff manual, the school places its emphasis on "a mixture of child initiated and teacher initiated learning that encourages divergent thinking and problem solving" where "children are empowered to plan what they will do, choose materials, and execute their plans with interested, involved adults facilitating." We have seen the operation of some of the classes where these goals are implemented, and we will look at more classes later. Let's take a look at the curriculum itself, what it seeks to accomplish and how it goes about meeting its goals. *At this point it would be instructive to examine the Rosa Lee Young curriculum outline itself, reprinted in Appendix A, and refer to it whenever appropriate.*

BUILDING THE IMPORTANT S-A-Ts IN CHILDREN: SEPARATION, AUTONOMY, TRUST

In an interesting footnote to the toddler curriculum, the school provides an insight into its primary tasks with toddlers that is in sharp contrast with the anxieties recently created over getting children ready for tests. An article in its house newsletter published for parents is titled *Toddlers Work on Their SATs*. But the SATs referred to here are the things that are really vital to the development of toddlers—separation, autonomy, and trust—and should thus be uppermost on the agendas of early childhood educators who work with children below the age of 3.

Separation, one of the most important of life's skills, is one of the first hurdles with which a toddler must learn to cope. It is the act of parting, even temporarily, with a loved one, and it hits little ones very hard. We described in Chapter 1 how a toddler teacher, Pepper Robinson, handled this act of separation. It was not something that came suddenly or by some formula but through mutual respect and trust that had been built among child, school, and parent each day. The article in the newsletter previously cited summed it up. Separation is "unique for each child and each family" and is recognized as such by the toddler teachers at Rosa Lee Young who try to make saying goodbye to parents each day "a healthy and emotionally positive experience." To do this, they strive to validate children's feelings and try to give children the words to describe their feelings. One way this is done with very young children is to help them have a "piece of home—whether a picture, a familiar item, or song—until they are able to hold Mommy or Daddy in their own minds." They are working on separation, the article pointed out, when they wave goodbye at the window.

Autonomy and independence should be encouraged by any day care program. Classrooms should be set up so young children can do things by themselves. Sinks, soap and water, and paper towels at toddler height enable the toddler to learn to wash her hands by herself. Coat hooks and cubbies in easy-to-reach places with the child's name on them help her to learn to put her own things away. All this comes with patience and time, as long as the idea is there and the program is set up for it.

Finally, as we have seen, building trust is the big task that early childhood educators must seek to accomplish—the child's trust that this setting and the people who care for her will love her and make her secure. Routines are kept simple and consistent, building the confidence in toddlers that the same things happen every day and that Mommy or Daddy will be coming "soon after rest time" to pick them up. The school and the toddler teacher strive to "get to know each family" and for the families to get to know them. The foundation of trust that we discussed at such great length in Chapter 2 is probably the most important foundation for a good child care program and must be kept at the forefront in setting up a curriculum in early child care.

LEARNING BY HANDS-ON EXPERIENCE

As far as cognitive learning at all levels is concerned, in the same newsletter issue Joan Sheppard, the school's director at that time, pointed out what a visitor should look for in any early child care program. "When you come to Rosa Lee Young," she wrote, "look for the learning taking place in different areas of the rooms. Because we know that preschool children construct their knowledge of the world around them by experiencing hands-on activities, our environment is rich with opportunities." Children "learn to interpret and represent their world in symbolic languages through drawing, painting, clay modeling, collage, dance, music, puppetry, and dramatic play. They can express their thoughts to attentive adults who then engage them in meaningful dialogue." They are provided with playdough, Legos, beads, and writing tools that stimulate both their fine motor skills and their imaginations. Songs, finger plays, stories, and games with rhyming words and alliteration create a literacy-rich environment to help them develop an understanding that words consist of a combination of sounds and that these sounds are represented by the words in books. Objects that encourage them to compare, contrast, sort, make patterns and sets, increase, and decrease, develop concepts necessary for mathematical thinking.[75] As pointed out earlier, the school here is taking its cue from the Reggio Emilia concept of child care, centering the activities of the children around their creative instincts and abilities.

Children develop creativity as they create and draw; play restaurant with menus and order blanks in the family corner; or create a town with roads, bridges, and buildings in the block corner. Learning is age appropriate—a vital element to keep in mind in this time of rote drilling for tests, beginning even with very young children, that is occurring in so many places. This kind of learning builds the foundation for the more structured learning that takes place as the child advances to elementary school and is a wonderful model for what a program for young children should be.

STAFF DEVELOPMENT IS AN ONGOING PROCESS

In every discussion of curriculum and practice, the question always returns to the quality of the staff and how well prepared staff members are to work in the field. As we have seen previously, the general state of early child care throughout the nation is far from adequate. "Today's reality," laments an article in the organ of one of the leading professional organizations in the field, "is that even with increased commitments to early care and education from the federal government and states, quality remains embarrassingly poor, staff salaries are inadequate, and high quality care is not affordable for most parents despite increasing subsidies. To say the least, there is no coherent system of care in the United States."[76]

Inservice training has, therefore, become extremely important in attaining professional staff competence in early childhood education. Indeed, as one child care administrator noted several years ago, "In early childhood, post-employment training takes on enormous importance since it is too often needed to help staff achieve minimum competency levels rather than to build their advanced skills. Employers and regulatory agencies turn to inservice training, such as conferences, with the expectation—or at least the hope—that participants will learn vital information in short periods of time."[77]

In the face of this, we know that despite the obstacles created by the enormous lack of funding and the absence of such a coherent system of early child

Solving a problem in the construction corner.

care in our country, there are good early child care centers with high-quality professional staffs. We have been writing about one of them, and we noted in Chapter 1 that the staff at Rosa Lee Young has been both educationally quali- fied and relatively stable. Over the years several have held a master's degree in early childhood education, and most others have held a bachelor's or associ- ate's degree. But it remains a struggle, particularly in this day of rising costs, to keep high-quality people in such low paying jobs. And, as in any profession, particularly one as sensitive to human development as this one, the training cannot stop there. There must be a system of inservice training that is relevant to the practical work being done by teachers in the classroom, not for "achiev- ing minimum competency skills," as noted earlier, but to maintain and build advanced skills among already qualified professionals. And it must also be affordable to them because their salaries often cannot keep up with the high tuition costs of most colleges today.

Some Principles of Inservice Training

Recognizing the importance of ongoing staff development, an article pub- lished in the *Zero to Three* journal several years ago outlined a few basic princi- ples an early child care center should follow in its inservice program. They may be outlined as follows:

1. *Staff development must be a process, not an event.* Too often inservice train- ing takes the form of a speaker or a discussion session that is a "one-shot deal." Someone comes in and lectures on a topic, there are some ques- tions and some discussion, and the session ends. Period. Much of the time the speaker is soon forgotten in the practical day-to-day problems that teachers face, about which the session addressed perhaps only peripherally. Staff development should not be handled in this way. All training should be part of the process of forwarding the goals of the child care program and should give the staff a sense of the basic per- spectives of the child care center. This is essential because staff members should clearly understand the philosophy and the goals of the program in which they work. For example, at one staff conference at Rosa Lee Young in the late spring, I was an invited guest speaker and presented a talk on what constitutes a high-quality child care program. I encour- aged staff members to evaluate their year's work with this in mind, and they engaged in a rich discussion of the goals of the program and how their work fit into it. They were able to see their strengths and weak- nesses and problems that needed attention and made practical sugges- tions to be carried over into the next year.

Training sessions like this have to be continually followed up to be effective. One way Rosa Lee Young does this is to encourage peer discussions of their work, at lunch or other gatherings, where they share ideas and critiques. *But staff self-evaluation, as we have described here, can never be successful if the second element, following, is not an integral part of the supervisor-teacher relationship at a school.*

2. *Teachers must feel completely safe in talking about their work.* In many schools, from early child care through secondary school, teachers are hesitant to seek the help of supervisors and administrators because they feel that any weakness on their part will be regarded as poor performance and could possibly threaten their jobs. Teachers will seek the help of supervisors only if the supervision is nonpunitive, and if they truly feel the supervisor is a partner in helping them to achieve success with the children. "A supervisory or mentoring system which reflects the precepts that 'supervision is a relationship for learning' and 'supervision should feel like help' is one of the most effective possible supports for professional development."[78] If such an atmosphere is created, supervision can be used to complement and follow up inservice training.

This is one of the great strengths of Rosa Lee Young, where, as teacher Linda Schnitzer pointed out, "The training here is ongoing." No matter what your level of preparation has been, "if you work in this school, you are required to have a certain number of hours of training per year." In addition, she noted, "Staff meetings and team meetings discuss children and their specific needs." At monthly staff meetings, even though an agenda is followed, there is always time when the floor is open for faculty discussion of problems and how to deal with them. "We've had some really interesting staff meetings where we've talked about strategies, where we've broken up into groups and played the roles of children in different situations" and discussed the best ways to deal with that situation. They talked about aspects of our curriculum, constantly evaluating it "to see if it's right. We've had staff meetings devoted to helping parents to know our philosophy" and fostering parent-teacher communication and cooperation. The key to it all, Schnitzer maintained, is that "the administration is so supportive" and that a cooperative atmosphere is encouraged among the entire staff. It's "a big piece of Rosa Lee Young," she said appreciatively.

My own observation as a guest speaker at one of their staff meetings bears this out. With the school's director, Jeannine Rey, present, teachers engaged in open discussion of their strengths and weaknesses without fear or hesitation. This can take place only in an atmosphere of complete trust among colleagues who do not fear that an administration is punitive but is genuinely there to help them become better teachers.

3. *Inservice training and supervision must seek to build skills in developing relations between the professional staff and the children's families.* Families are, after all, the central focus of the child's attitudes and the things he learns. There is often a gap between the staff and the parents that is aggravated by many things such as culture, class, and professional status. This gap must be overcome if a healthy atmosphere is to prevail in any educational institution, particularly one that serves young children. An appropriate inservice program should include discussions on how to help the staff build relationships with the families of the children in their care.

4. *An inservice program should adhere to the principle of scaffolding.* The idea of scaffolding knowledge, of building on the strengths one already has, is important in staff development. A program of ongoing training should start with the strengths of the program and the staff and move forward from there. "By shining the light on individual and program strengths, we can help staff understand that they have a strong foundation upon which to build new skills and practices. We also draw attention to the resources available for moving the process forward. . . . When a new concept or practice is presented in the context of what is already happening, we communicate an appreciation and respect for staff competence and skills. This, in turn, helps to build the trust needed for staff to consider making a change." And, of course, "staff needs to trust that management has a realistic understanding of the demands of the work, and will provide adequate resources" (including time and assistance with the implementation of new approaches).[79]

5. *Staff development should stress how to understand and use developmentally appropriate practices with children.* All children, but particularly young children, go through different stages that requires a variety of approaches in working with them. Too often, teaching methods appropriate only for older children are used that can be destructive in younger children. All staff development must emphasize the methods appropriate with the different age groups of children in the program and how each teacher must use the methods that connect with the age groups of his particular class (see Appendix A).

In one prekindergarten class at Rosa Lee Young, the children took care of a pet, a guinea pig they named Miss Piggy, for the entire school year. It excited them as they watched it run on a treadmill, and they made sure it was fed and given water each day. That was one of the regular jobs rotated among the children on a daily basis. It was the job no one forgot. It was the most sought-after task in the class as children could not wait until it was their turn to feed and water Miss Piggy. Sometimes they would gather round as the teacher brought it out and let it run around in a larger enclosure on the floor. They often took turns petting its fur and sometimes during the day one of the children would be seen talking to it through its cage.

This was not a haphazard event in the class, or one thought up by a teacher looking for an activity for the children. It was part of the regular curriculum, as noted in Appendix A. In taking care of their guinea pig, they were observing it, learning about animals and the foods that sustain them, describing them, writing about them, and drawing them.

But they were also learning something else. They were learning how to be gentle with other living things, how to be caring and loving. They were learning how to cooperate with their fellow classmates in the care of a life. Their emotions were developing along with their thinking and reasoning.

"Look at this!" Fun in the family corner.

And that is the real objective of early child care. To develop a human being in many ways. To prepare him for more complex learning, and to begin the process that makes him able to feel love, warmth, cooperation, and understanding for the world and the life around him. It's no accident. It's all planned, part of a well-thought-out curriculum that is an essential part of any good child care program, administered by teachers who are well-trained and continually updated in their craft.

What to Consider in Creating a Good Curriculum for Early Child Care

The curriculum of the Rosa Lee Young Child Care program is reproduced in Appendix A. Each child care program will shape its own curriculum based upon its own particular needs and resources. However, in drawing up its curriculum, each program should keep the following goals for the children in mind.

Develop Skills by Participating With the Entire Class

1. Listening skills: acquiring the ability to understand ideas experienced in stories, poems, and other reading materials

2. Discussion skills: acquiring the ability to talk about the stories they have heard

3. Dramatization skills: acquiring the ability to grasp the sequence of a story, act it out, work as a team on playing it, and use their imaginations to make up their own stories

4. Music and movement skills: learning to sing and react to songs and stories using body and dance movements to express ideas; learning about musical instruments

Develop Skills Through Individual Play or Through Play in Small Groups

1. Painting and drawing: using art media (paint, crayons, paper, staplers, scissors, etc.) to illustrate their experiences. This use of art can support the child's learning experiences in areas like science, math, and language comprehension.

2. Construction projects: also supporting their experiences in other areas

3. Reading and writing skills: using drawing to represent a letter or word (an apple for *a*, a ball for *b*, etc.)

4. Listening and writing: creating a class book by telling the teacher a story as she writes it down

5. Learning through role playing: playing at being a mommy or daddy; grocery shopping; ordering in a restaurant; paying at a cash register; playing policeman, fireman, mailman, doctor, teacher, and other roles

6. Math skills: learning the concept of numbers, measurements, spatial relationships, addition and subtraction; for example, preparing foods by learning how to measure ingredients

7. Social skills: learning to negotiate, share, take turns, be empathetic toward others, regulate behavior

8. Science skills: learning to observe what causes things to occur (such as an ice cube melting in warm air), observing and caring for pets, collecting information on insects and talking about it, learning about weather and seasons, displaying the information they collect on a science bulletin board

9. Manipulation skills: acquiring eye-hand coordination through construction with blocks, Legos, and other equipment; learning through touch about different textures

10. Gross motor skills: jumping, running, climbing, ball playing (playground activities); skipping, hopping, body movement, dance (indoor activities)

11. Emotional development: learning how to control feelings by expressing them verbally rather than through physical aggression toward another person

(Continued)

Continued

Develop Special Toddler Skills

1. Playing with water and sand to enhance sensory motor skills
2. Learning how to express feelings and control negative behavior
3. Simple manipulation skills: playing with toys that teach size, shape, and texture; establishing relationships; putting caps on bottles; putting on hats, socks, shoes
4. Art skills: using crayons, sponges, finger paints, and other materials
5. Handling separation from parents each day
6. Learning how to listen to stories, sing, and explore different body movements
7. Engaging in symbolic play
8. Learning social skills in groups, such as empathy with others and taking turns

Some Questions on Staff Training

1. Is there an ongoing process of inservice training for the staff?
2. Is the principal focus of training and staff conferences on improving the teaching skills of the staff, or is it heavily concentrated on administrative matters?
3. Do teachers and administrators maintain a professional attitude toward their work? Do teachers regard administrators as people who are there to improve their work? Do teachers have the confidence that they can bring problems to their administrators without fear of retribution?

The School as a Reflection of Our Diverse Heritage

The Rosa Lee Young Childhood Center is committed to providing high-quality education and care for children from economically, ethnically, and racially diverse families in and around Rockville Centre.

—Mission Statement of the Rosa Lee Young Childhood Center

Too often, parents look for a school or a class that reflects only their own images. But American society is rich in the diversity of its people and cultures. Teaching children respect for this diversity can best be accomplished if the children, from their earliest years, come across this diversity in their own experience, to the greatest extent possible in any community. A school that believes in this principle can make the diverse cultures of its children into a natural experience. This chapter describes

- How an ethnically diverse student body in a child care center can be an asset in the development of the children as they learn about different cultures and races in a friendly, positive way
- How the school curriculum can make the diverse cultures of the children a daily living experience
- How children speaking different languages can be an asset in the classroom and how non-English speaking students can be made to feel a part of the class in the process of learning English
- How the cultural diversity of our society can be reflected in the stories the children read, the games they play, and the foods they eat
- How the celebration of holidays can reflect the diverse character of our society
- How ethnic stereotypes may be countered in young children and how they can learn to experience friendship without excluding someone because he is "different"
- Why it is important for staff members to reflect upon their own backgrounds and attitudes about different cultures in the process of working with the children

The chapter also discusses some difficulties that may arise in working with families of different cultural backgrounds and preferences, and how such difficulties may be overcome.

The kids call her "Grandma." She moves from class to class and is inevitably greeted with warmth and delight when she enters the room. She speaks to the children in English and Spanish, and she has helped two of the teachers develop a Spanish-English language program for their prekindergarten/kindergarten class. For the English-speaking children in the class, they are learning a second language at an age when educational researchers say they can learn it most easily, as very young children. For Spanish-speaking children, it is helping them to function and learn in a culture in which proficiency in English is essential for future success.

For Rosa Lee Young, Maria Del Valle is a local treasure, the "foster grandparent" to the children. She came originally from the Nassau County Department of Senior Citizen Affairs, Foster Grandparent program. She is a senior volunteer who has spent her time at the school enriching the experience of the children. She told the *Rockville Centre Herald* in November 2005 that Rosa Lee Young was like family to her and a nice place for kids.[80] Fluent in the two languages, she has helped to make children coming from different cultures comfortable in a setting that recognizes and builds on the dignity of each child's cultural background. An educational experience of this kind is priceless.

One of the most important tasks of education is to prepare young people for life in the real world. That real world, particularly in our country, is a complex one filled with ever-changing ideas, rapid technological growth, and, most important of all, a highly diverse population from many different backgrounds and cultures.

The children at Rosa Lee Young, proudly noted the school's director, Jeannine Rey, have an advantage right from the beginning of making friends with children from many backgrounds. "They're seeing America, and America is diverse. Long Island is diverse, and New York certainly is. It's where we are, so why shouldn't our early childhood centers look that way?"

This has been the philosophy of the school from the very beginning. Joan Sheppard, who was the school's director for twenty-five years, was quite emphatic about this point. "Children need to see children from other backgrounds, and what better time to do this than when they are young children!" she observed. Racial, cultural, and class differences are minimal among them. "'If he has a smile and I want to play with him, then he's my friend.' We believed that was where it should begin."

But it wasn't always easy. "Unfortunately," she recalled, "we met up with parents who did not believe in that and wanted their children in all white programs. But there still were a lot who liked what we were doing," who believed in the school's philosophy that as children play together every day, it helps to dispel some of the stereotypes that develop as children grow. Joan recounted stories of friendships made at Rosa Lee Young among children of different backgrounds that lasted well beyond their stay at the school and carried over for years afterward. That's how people learn about other people, she emphasized, and that's what the school's philosophy is all about.

Or as Jeannine Rey put it, "We learn together, we play together, we have fun together, we have families. They're different. They're the same." From an early age, "it dispels some of the notions and fears about others."

At the same time, it is important for children of all groups to feel that they are not alone. A single African American or Hispanic or white child in a classroom is not the answer to providing a diverse student setting for children. Jeannine recounts an incident involving a little girl whose mother was from the Philippines and whose father was white from the United States. The girl looked more Filipino than white. A member of the school's board of directors, a woman of Chinese descent, once came in and visited the classroom. "The little girl took the board member by the face with her hands on either side of her cheeks," Jeannine recalled, "and said, 'You have my face.'"

The incident was very significant, she feels, because it reflected the fact that "we don't have very many Asian children in our center. We have had some Asian children—Korean children, Chinese children, Filipino children—but we don't have a large Asian population in Rockville Centre or the surrounding communities. This child didn't see herself reflected in the community at the school. When she saw someone who looked like her, this 3-year-old was immediately aware of this and was filled with delight. 'You look like me,' she was saying. For that child and for all children, I think it is very important to see yourself reflected in the school community around you." It gives children a sense of belonging, of being a part of a community.

"A child's roots are held deep within the cultural context of family and community," noted material presented at a national conference on child care. "As the child grows and spreads out into the wider world, his roots stay planted firmly within that culture. He learns language and how to communicate first from his parents, which is further supported by what he hears and his interactions within the community."[81] Our children are the product of their diverse cultures. When they inevitably meet in the real world of school and adulthood, it is essential for our nation's well-being that they are secure in their own culture and appreciate each other's cultural heritage while they share the common values of American society.

And this should begin at a very young age.

But, although the school administration is aware of the importance of a diverse student body and has paid close attention to trying to maintain an ethnic

Engrossed in a computer game.

balance among the children, administrators have never turned anyone away because it would upset some numerical balance. "We're aware of it. We talk about it. A balance is important to us," said Jeannine, "but the families that show up at our doorstep that need the service we provide are the families we serve." At the same time, they are conscious of the question and the results are classes that strongly resemble the people these children will meet when they grow up and emerge into adult American society. This is a healthy part of their training, provided the staff of the child care center knows how to use this diversity as a strength rather than viewing it as a liability and a source of problems.

DIVERSITY AS A NATURAL PART OF THE CURRICULUM

With young children a major goal in their educational development is to encourage the growth of positive images about people in their minds. "We have images about people," observed Jeannine. "What causes us to have the images that we do? It's where we live and what we've seen and it's the other images that are portrayed in society at large—TV, movies, and, so forth." That's why teachers should be aware of the literature they're bringing into the classroom for the children. "Who's in them? What kind of stories are they? Who are the people? What do the faces look like? What's the family composition?" She thought back to the images presented to children of what a family was like when she was growing up. The stereotypical family in the fifties and sixties was personified by the television series *Father Knows Best* and similar portrayals where Mom kept the home fires burning, took care of the children's little problems, and always managed to look gorgeous all day, whereas dad went off to the office with his suit and tie and his briefcase. They were always white, and there was always a house with a picket fence around the yard. "What are the images we are exposing children to in things like literature?" Jeannine asked. Of course, there are families like this, and they should be part of the picture, but she maintains that teachers must be aware that children's cultural activities should also show families in which Mom works and Dad is a factory worker or a school teacher or a plumber. And, of course, the families of different races should also be there for children to see.

Rosa Lee Young gives a lot of attention to this real diversity of American culture, but it's usually so much a natural part of its regular routine that you barely notice it. First of all, and most important, the school itself is an integrated community with staff, children, and parents constantly interacting with each other. Mothers and fathers walk through the door every day with their children, and staff members greet them and talk with them. The atmosphere is casual and friendly, and the children see this. The children—a cross-section of class, race, and culture—are consistently interacting with each other all day long. "To me, that's the biggest thing," emphasized Jeannine. "The way they play. The way they talk together. The way adults talk to children." The children are encouraged to use language to communicate their ideas, feelings, needs, desires, and fears. "What you want young children to do is to communicate their personal experiences. Young children can communicate a wealth of experiences when they're encouraged to do so. They talk about their families, their celebrations, the places they go with their families, the food they eat together."

Bringing the Children's Languages Into the Classroom

But, of course, that has to be just the beginning. There has to be a conscious effort to bring the rich cultural experiences of the children and their families directly into the curriculum. For example, we mentioned that in one class, Maria Del Valle, the senior volunteer known affectionately as "Grandma," helped set up a Spanish-English language program. That was the prekindergarten/kindergarten class of Lisa Streb and Sally Ann Braman. Grandma and the teachers did this by putting pictures of objects on the floor and then playing games with them, like saying their names in English and Spanish. In one variation of this game, the children took turns as a child went to a different part of the room and another child removed one of the pictures. The child came in and had to guess which picture had been removed by saying its name in Spanish and English. They also taught the children some songs in Spanish, made and named foods from Hispanic recipes, and read books about people from Hispanic cultures.

"In 1991, 38 percent of the three- to five-year-old preschoolers in our country who lived in homes in which a language other than English was the primary language participated in center-based early childhood programs," reported a study published by the Office of Educational Research and Improvement of the U.S. Department of Education and cited in a leading scholarly journal. It predicted, at that time, that "by the year 2000, about five million preschoolers in the United States would be from families speaking a language other than English."[82] Zero to Three cautions that this can present a real challenge to teachers who face these children.

> Language is embedded in a culture and is one of the most powerful ways in which culture is expressed and shaped. Culture provides young children with a sense of identity and a frame of reference that helps them understand their world. Any message, however subtle, that devalues the children's language and culture has profound impact on their sense of being and their relationship with their family and community. . . . Young children receive powerful messages about home and self from the language they hear, see and are encouraged to use. Very early on, children receive messages about belonging and being accepted. These extend to the expectations that teachers and larger society share about what "language/culture" is acceptable and valued. Therein lies the danger. When young children are asked to "leave their home language and culture at the classroom door," they may learn that their home language and culture is not important and may actually be barriers to being successful. In this case, young children may lose their

A Great Discovery—She Spoke!

During the free activities time in one of the prekindergarten classes while children were playing with large construction blocks, bathing ducks at the water table, spray painting with shaving cream mixed with colors, and attending to dolls in the family area, the following scene took place:

> Two boys, Ronnie and Jason, are playing at the water table. Nearby, Anna, a Spanish-speaking girl who only recently joined the class, is wheeling a doll around in a shopping cart. Anna, who knows only a little English, is still unsure of herself and hardly as yet talks to the other children. Ronnie suddenly splashes water on his clothes.

Ronnie: My mommy's going to get mad at me.

Jason: My mommy said I could do this.

Ronnie (holding two plastic ducks and talking to them): You're scared. You can bang your head. (With another voice mimicking a duck) I'm not scared.

Jason: Let's play six little ducks. (He begins singing the song "Six Little Ducks" and Ronnie joins in. The song is obviously very familiar to both of them.)

Six little ducks that I once knew,

Fat ones, skinny ones, fair ones, too.

But the one little duck with the feather on his back

He led the others with a quack, quack, quack.

Ronnie (still holding the ducks): I'm feeding poopie.

(Anna then comes by wheeling the doll in the shopping cart and wheels it directly into the bathroom. A teacher sees her, goes after her, and brings her out.

Jason (referring to Anna): She's shopping for water.

Anna (to her doll): Sleep, baby.

Ronnie (astounded): You spoke!

home language in order to gain acceptance. However, this occurs at a great cost. With the loss of home language, young children may also lose a sense of cultural identity, heritage, and most importantly, the support and wisdom of their family members."[83]

For an early child care center, it means that, as we have already noted, the staff must be aware of the differences in the cultural backgrounds of the children, be sensitive to them, and build on them so that they strengthen their program. And it should come naturally, not some superimposed bit of pop cultural material that's thrown in once in a while, often to celebrate some holiday.

Using Holidays to Celebrate Cultural Diversity

Which brings us to another point: the way school holidays are handled. Like most child care centers, Rosa Lee Young takes advantage of school holidays to celebrate the cultural heritage of Americans. But in most places, the celebration of Thanksgiving, for example, consists of pictures of turkeys and construction of Pilgrim hats and Indian headdress. Back in the eighties, this bothered the school administration a bit. Joan Sheppard was the director and she discussed it with the staff. Thanksgiving was essentially a North American holiday, they reasoned, so perhaps the Hispanic families, whose children were then beginning to come into the school, might not feel included. These days we often poke fun at being politically correct, and sometimes well-meaning people carry it to some silly excesses, but I feel that it is far better to err on the side of some occasional foolishness than not to be conscious of the need to be sensitive to the cultural heritages of the many groups that make up our country. At any rate, the concern of the school that some of its students might not feel the same way about Thanksgiving prompted the school administration to send home a family questionnaire on the holiday—how they celebrated it, the food they ate, and the activities they engaged in. Most of the families returned the questionnaire. What a surprise the school administration got when they read the responses from the Hispanic families. What did they eat on Thanksgiving? Why, turkey, of course. They usually served it with rice and beans and plantains instead of sweet potatoes, but the big bird was a feature on the family table with Dad usually doing the carving honors. What, of course, was most important was that the Thanksgiving holiday for Hispanic families, as for most families in America, was a *family* holiday, a time when families gather to enjoy each other, to laugh, and to marvel at how the children have grown and how smart they are.

Foods, Families, and Culture

And so, the children at Rosa Lee Young—white, black, Hispanic, Jewish, Christian, or whatever—celebrate Thanksgiving by talking about their families, what they do, the foods on the table, the people they saw, and the toys they played with. In place of the patterned artwork, the Indian feathered head bands, and the Pilgrim hats, they read stories about Native American children in North America that serve to dispel some of the classical myths about them. They shape "food" out of playdough to simulate the Thanksgiving food they ate at home. There is a great emphasis on food because it is so central to the experience of young children and it is such a good vehicle for learning about how different people do different things. We have mentioned in an earlier chapter how, in the prekindergarten class of Linda Schnitzer and Vanessa Weiss-Barkofsky at Rosa Lee Young, there was a unit on bread in which the children listened and read stories about breads from around the world and then mixed the ingredients and baked Irish soda bread, Jewish challah bread, English muffins, Italian and French bread, and others. This, it turns out, is not an isolated experience confined to one classroom. Native foods from countries around the world, particularly the foods eaten by children in the class, give the children the chance to talk about their foods, homes, and families; make children of varied backgrounds feel at home; and give all the children a sense and appreciation of the variety of cultures in their midst. And because bread is so much a part of the staple food of many cultures, it is used in many class-rooms as a means of having children discuss their experiences at home. On Thanksgiving or other holiday occasions, the children can be seen pounding away at their playdough to make "flat breads" or shaping it around their fin-gers to make "bagels" or molding it into "rye" or "whole wheat" or long, thin Italian loaves. On the Jewish holiday of Passover, they sometimes distribute pieces of *matzoh* as a snack and talk about how it is eaten by Jewish people in celebration of their holiday.

And on Thanksgiving the older children in the prekindergarten and kinder-garten classes prepare real foods with their teachers—pies and mashed pota-toes and rice and anything that the children remember from their tables at home that is feasible to prepare in their school setting. The oven in the kitchen is kept busy, and holiday food is made and shared with other classes in the school. Now that's an experience worth remembering because instead of a stereotypi-cal event that young children really do not understand, the children see a diver-sity of experience that the children of different cultural groups bring with them to the school, and each of them shares in the experience. For in the end, we all celebrate Thanksgiving. We all have families. We may eat some foods that are different and some that are the same, but we all have a lot in common.

Even with musical instruments in the classroom, the school tries to reflect a broad cultural experience. Young children love percussion instruments, they love to bang on something and have musical tones come out. The school tries to use musical instruments from different cultures. In addition to the drums and bells, for example, they found that kids love "rain sticks" from South America, an instrument formed from hollowed-out cactus with the needles inside. When two of them are hit together, it sounds like rain falling. Of course, the children here are very young and they still have no idea of the place they're in as part of a larger city or country or world, so Jeannine tries to have these instruments in the classroom as part of a normal environment, and children use them as a matter of course—they're part of the play routine. Children pick them up, play them, and get to experience them the way they experience most other things during the school day. Later on, they'll hear about the places these things come from and they'll get the connection.

What the school is trying hard to do, explained Jeannine, is to "make diver-sity normal." People from many cultures come into the school and are seen by the children all the time. Tjuana, the cook, often wears African scarves. When the kids in the toddler room see them, Jeannine said, they often try to imitate them by putting colorful scarves on themselves, the way they would dress up in Mommy's high heels or Daddy's baseball cap. "Children imitate adults around them. That's how they learn. That's why we have family corners and the trucks and the baby dolls and the things that look like the stuff around them." And their seeing and using the various objects of many cultures is part of this philosophy of making cultural diversity just a normal part of the classroom.

Jeannine recalled the time this led to some criticism from a visitor representing a national organization. The visitor had come to see the program at Rosa Lee Young. She was impressed with the school but criticized the way it handled the matter of cultural diversity. "She wanted us to have more proplike things" like a specific African colored cloth that children could put on, and regular celebrations of holidays from other countries. "Well, we try to do it differently. It's true, we don't celebrate Cinco de Mayo.[84] What does that mean to young children? That's not to say it won't be mentioned. We also sometimes mention the Chinese New Year and have taught the children the Chinese words *gung hay fat choy*, the traditional Chinese New Year greeting." But she pointed to a number of books by early childhood educators cautioning against "taking the tourist approach to learning about cultures—like Mexican hat dances, and whatever. Of course, you'll see some of our older kids learning that, but we're careful about how we portray other cultures and what they do and what their holidays are." Africans, for example, wear many things. Some wear traditional costumes and some wear Western-style business suits. And most Mexicans don't go around doing hat dances all day. Sometimes these things you do in the name of presenting to children the cultures of other people can be very disrespectful. "We're careful about how we portray other cultures and what they do and what their holidays are. Just because you've used some of these props or taught a Mexican dance doesn't mean you've educated anybody about who those people really are. We have to be very careful about stereotyping."

Working With Families of Different Cultural Preferences

I mentioned in a previous chapter that the school's social worker, Barbara Andrzejewski, discusses the possibility of family observance of dietary laws for religious reasons in her initial interview with parents. But that's just the beginning. There is also the need to ascertain the family's cultural preferences about other things. Rosa Lee Young has had families who were Jehovah's Witnesses, whose religion forbids celebrations, flag salutes, and other ceremonial events. It is important to accommodate these things that are important to the family, but we must be aware that the child who has a different custom or eats a different food must be made to feel just as at home as any of the other children. This is often a difficult task. "When you are eating a different food from everyone else at the table or you can't come to a birthday party or you can't be in the room if there is a pledge of allegiance, this is very difficult for you to understand in the larger context of culture if you're a little kid," Jeannine noted. "In the case of the child of a Jehovah's Witness family, if there was a celebration like a birthday party, we would have it in the afternoon and try to make arrangements to have the child picked up early. If they couldn't do that, we would find a subtle way to have the child join another class for a time. It wasn't completely comfortable for us and not every situation was resolved happily for the child but we would try. What is most important of all, we have to talk about it with the child and the parent, not just once but all the time because we want that child not to feel uncomfortable because she is different in a certain way from the other children."

HANDLING ETHNIC STEREOTYPES AMONG CHILDREN

An interesting sidelight on this question is the way the staff has been trained to respond to remarks that children sometimes make about other children they perceive to be different. After all, by the time a child gets to the prekindergarten level at the age of 3 or 4, he has heard some people around him talking. They don't necessarily have to be his parents. A child is remarkably adept at absorbing conversations he has heard in a variety of places. and he has begun to become aware of some differences among children.

"Do we ever hear stereotypical things coming out of the mouths of some of our children?" Jeannine asked. "Yes, we do. But we have an opportunity here. First of all, we don't blast them for it because they really don't understand what they have said." Children often say things that sound terrible to adults who have had extensive experience with those things in the world we know. What the teacher has to do here is to take a step back and look at the child. When a child is upset with another child, he will often pick at the thing he perceives as different about that child. He will find it even at the age of 3, Jeannine noted, and it's usually something obvious. It could be if a child cries a lot or if his skin

**"Teddy Bear Day." Children brought their teddy
bears to school to share the day with them.**

is of a different color or if he goes to a different church. So instead of saying, "I don't want to play with you because you take my toys," he'll say, "I don't want to play with you because your skin is brown." And even though a child's remark of this nature can be very upsetting to teachers, teachers have to be trained to get to the bottom of what the child is really upset about and separate it from the stereotype. Showing the child the difference between the two is a very valuable part of his education.

Jeannine related a story of two children, one Christian, one Jewish. The Jewish child knew about the myth of Santa Claus, but the Christian child still had this as a belief. In an ensuing discussion, the Jewish child told the Christian child that Santa Claus was not real. "Your mommy and your daddy give you those presents," he insisted. And the Christian child turned around and said, "You're not my friend because you're Jewish." The parents of both children were upset when they heard about it because, from the adult point of view, they understood the consequences of remarks like this. Jeannine remembers telling the parents that they had to understand what was going on between the two kids. "It has nothing to do with what you think it does. One child was really saying to the other, 'You're causing me stress. I don't like what you're saying to me, you hurt me and I know that you're Jewish.' That's what he was seeing right at that moment. If this had never happened no one would have cared who was Jewish and who was Christian."

Of course, a situation like this cannot be ignored. To ignore it is to perhaps allow it to fester, and educators would not be doing their jobs if they did not deal with it. But, Jeannine emphasized that teachers should be trained not to react with shock or horror but must help children get to the bottom of the issue. She illustrated her point with an imaginary dialogue between teacher and child.

> "You just told Robert you're not his friend (or you didn't want to play with him or you don't like him or whatever the statement). Why? What are you upset about?"

> "He took my toy (or he says mean things to me or he pinches me or something)."

> "Oh, so you must tell him that you're not playing with him because you don't want him to hurt you (or say mean things to you)" (And to the other child) "Do you remember hurting him (or saying something to him he doesn't like)? He's telling you he doesn't want you to do that."

"The purpose," declared Jeannine, "is to get the kids to talk to each other, to tell each other what's really bothering them, to get at what the issue is—in other words, to get them to communicate. That's a lot of what *doesn't* go on in the world. People do not communicate over their real differences, so it becomes the obvious difference between them—race, religion, ethnic differences—and that's what we end up attacking instead of the real underlying factor that's causing the problem." But if we start asking children to confront this at a young age, and if it's followed through as the child grows older, we hope it can play a role in solving problems like this later on in life. But it can best be accomplished over the long run in an atmosphere in which children see an appreciation for the cultural diversity of others in a natural setting as part of their everyday experience.

CULTURAL DIVERSITY AND DIFFERING EXPECTATIONS

A multicultural student body in an early child care center can present another issue that the staff must be prepared to face. All of us are the products of our culture, and this culture, though invisible to us most of the time, is "the framework for our lives. It includes our food, clothing, furniture, art, games, and habits as well as our deep beliefs and values—the way we look at the world, the way we relate to one another and the way we bring up our children." It is like a second layer of skin that emerges into view only when we come across a culture that is different from our own.[85] When this happens, we tend to view the customs of others as somehow "incorrect." When it comes to child care, they sometimes don't conform to the expectations we have for children and the way we have been trained to work with them. Take, for example, an interesting case in point, the question of what parents regard as the goals of good parenting and education. All parents have goals and expectations for their children, but differences arise, among other reasons, "because societies have different expectations for members of their communities. For example, in many Western societies, including European-American traditions in the United States, there is an emphasis on people being independent, self-reliant, and self-assertive and a focus on individual achievement. In contrast, in many Asian and Latin American cultures, interdependence, cooperation, and collaboration are widely held values. Differences in these general cultural values or expectations for members of communities can lead to differences in the socialization goals and strategies that parents adopt for their children."[86]

Cultural differences are often reflected in the way young children behave toward their teachers, and these differences are invariably misunderstood by teachers who are not prepared for it. In one research survey, a teacher who was interviewed told of her experience in her first year of working with children from Latino families. "There were a lot of things I had to learn," she recalled. "Just the nature of the children, the things they would do differently, and the reasons behind it . . . [were] different from my culture." She described her expectation that when she spoke to children, she expected them to look her in the eye. She was always trained this way. It was something she expected, second nature to her, part of her culture. But she found that the Latino children in her class looked down when she spoke to them, and she couldn't understand why. Until she discovered that in the culture of the children, they were taught by their parents that a child looks down as a sign of respect for the teacher, a sign that the teacher is to be obeyed. Direct eye contact in the children's culture occurred among equals, not when the child is addressed by the teacher. It was just one of the many cultural misunderstandings that must be overcome in the training of teachers who work with children of different backgrounds.[87]

This cultural dichotomy can lead to differences in what some parents expect the goals of early child care to be and what the professional staff in an early child care center in the United States is trained to do when it comes to child development. "In China," according to one example, "teachers viewed shy, sensitive children as socially and academically competent. In North America, teachers viewed shy, sensitive children as lonely and depressed. In Sweden, shy, socially reserved behavior was not consistently associated with any negative long-term outcomes, yet in North America, such behavior was found to hinder careers."[88]

This question is further complicated when children of different cultures are mixed in a class and there are different expectations among parents of children in the same class of how the staff should be working with their children. The problem is significant. According to one article, nearly 40 percent of children in the United States are being raised in families whose socialization goals and values may differ from the "ideal traits" prized among Euro-American families. "In our diverse society," the study's authors asked, "how can we adapt our practices to best facilitate the development of these bicultural participants?"[89]

It may be difficult for some people to grasp, but as two child care authorities pointed out a few years ago, "there are no 'best' childrearing methods, no norms

Winter is no obstacle at the outdoor playground.

or expectations. Children naturally develop the characteristics that their own culture values. Emotional display and affect, moral development, gender roles, even cognitive abilities depend on what competencies the culture requires of its citizens." There is one standard, however, that all who rear or work with children should strive for: the importance "for children to develop a positive self-concept [and] the need and the right to feel good about themselves. What is less well known is that their culture is a vital part of that self-concept and that children also have the need and the right to be proud of their cultural heritage. Children begin to construct their identity—to understand who they are—from understanding their own culture and by responding to how others see and relate to them. To form a positive self-concept, children need to honor and respect their own culture and have others honor and respect it too. This is a vital human need. When we don't recognize a child's identity—or even when we misrecognize it— we can actually harm her by putting her self-concept at risk."[90]

Therefore, it is important to understand and appreciate cultural influences among people when we work with children of varied backgrounds because it enables us to breach a potential divide and communicate better with children and their parents. But, as child psychologist Alicia Lieberman strongly cautioned, "It is important to keep in mind that these are cultural tendencies" rather than something that is true of all people of any one group. All they really mean "is that on the average, it is more likely that a person from a given culture . . . will display more of a particular trait" than a person from another culture. *To make sweeping generalizations beyond this would not be cultural sensitivity, it would be stereotyping*" [emphasis mine].[91] It is also essential to bear in mind that "culture is fluid, existing within individuals and continuously modified in the context of social interactions . . . that cultural communities are also ever-changing. . . . Within any group, researchers will find wide variations in beliefs and practices based on individual experiences and interpretations."[92]

Working With Children of Different
Cultural Backgrounds: Some Helpful Hints

The professional journal *Young Children*, in an article a few years ago, gave early child care professionals some helpful suggestions in working with children of differing cultural backgrounds in their programs. Among their recommendations are the following:

1. Listen to parents and discuss things of mutual interest for their children in a friendly, nonjudgmental way. Listening and "sharing our perspectives is one way we can begin to understand individual families' goals for their children and the ways in which they try to help their children achieve these goals. Asking parents how we can complement their efforts, rather than telling them what they ought to be doing supports this type of communication." Some families' beliefs will be quite different from our own, and we can learn to appreciate these differences even as the parents come to appreciate the perspective of the school in working with the child.

2   When one child or several children speak a different language than the teacher speaks, or when children in the class speak several different languages, one way to help children adjust to the classroom is to learn immediately the correct pronunciation of each child's name and a few important words in the children's language or languages (like *eat, stop, bathroom, listen*). The teacher should also use a variety of gestures, drawings, and objects to make himself understood.

3. Allowing a non-English-speaking child to manipulate objects, draw, and play more at individual games by himself so he does not have to negotiate with other children whom he does not understand and who do not understand him offers him a breathing space during the day when he does not have to strain to communicate. Eventually, as his English improves, he can be eased slowly into activities that allow him to begin negotiation with the other children in the class. By the same token, if he is put into a group, it should be small so he can easily follow what other children are doing without necessarily understanding the words they are using. And by establishing classroom routines that are consistent, the teacher is helping him to participate in familiar activities each day as he learns the English words that go with the activity.

4. Ask parents about their child's favorite song in the child's home language. If the parent has a recording of the song, ask if you can tape a copy of it. If it is played in the classroom, it allows the teacher to bring to all the children the linguistic and cultural diversity of the class. It also could allow the child to gain confidence in her surroundings as she becomes an "expert," teaching the song to the other children. If the song can be translated, the teacher might then teach the children the song in English as well as in the child's language. Such an activity goes a long way to giving children an appreciation for other cultures.

5. Whether there are children in the class from different ethnic backgrounds, children could be given the opportunities to share their own family cultures with their classmates via family photographs (including the teacher's family) on bulletin boards or in a class book. Children can be encouraged to share with the other children something special about their homes and families—for example, their favorite books and music, or how they celebrate their holidays. Parents could also be invited into the class to add to the discussion.[93]

In short, an ethnically and culturally diverse student body, far from being a drawback to a child care center—or, for that matter, to any school—can be a source of strength and provide an outstanding educational experience for the children, *provided the administration and the staff understand and appreciate the strength of a multicultural educational setting and know how to use it.*

We all know that nothing in this world is perfect. The administrators and staff of Rosa Lee Young know that each day in this field brings new problems, particularly in light of the constant struggle for more adequate funding that haunts every program like this one. But a school in which the children present such a cross-section of America, a school in which the child of the doctor who heads the department of cardiology at a major hospital in the area joins hands at circle time with the child of a worker at Home Depot, a school in which the mixture of white, black, and brown children of many creeds and ethnic backgrounds gives it the look of a little United Nations, a school in which diversity is a natural, living, daily experience, is a school that must be doing something right.

How Does Your Child Care Program Take Advantage of America's Richly Diverse Cultural Heritage?

1. Does the child care center value the languages and cultures of the children in their care? Specifically: Does it teach the children words, songs, and customs of the cultures of different areas of the world, which eventually leads to a more productive and enriched environment? Do children see parents of the various cultures and ethnic groups welcomed at the school? Do the teachers bring to the class the various aspects of the cultures of the children—that is, the foods eaten at home, the holidays they celebrate, the songs that are sung? Is there an awareness of the role that families, cultures, and languages play in education?

2. Does the child care center make a central part of its program the link between home and school? Specifically: Does the classroom have pictures of the children's homes and families on display? Does the school, from time to time, invite parents to share their expertise on themes that relate to their specific cultures? Do parents understand the values taught to the children at school and how they compare with their own values so they can become aware of the differences and similarities, allowing them to make a connection between what the teachers are teaching at school and what the parents are teaching at home?

3. Do teachers use familiar culturally relevant literature in their classrooms? Do the books that are read show characters that are diverse in ethnicity, race, and class? Do they show positive story lines and images to help the children develop a healthy self-concept and favorable views of others?

4. Do teachers talk in class about cultural similarities and differences in a way that brings out the enriching experience that they are?

5. When parents express certain cultural preferences such as special foods to conform to dietary laws, is this handled in a way that does not create negative images of the child as "peculiar" but rather that each one of us is an individual and entitled to respect?

High-Quality Child Care as a Learning Experience

> *Play gives children a chance to practice what they are learning. . . . They have to play with what they know to be true in order to find out more, and then they can use what they learn in new forms of play.*
>
> —Fred Rogers
> Late TV personality
> *Mr. Rogers' Neighborhood*

> *Children need time to stare at a wall, daydream over a picture book, make mud pies, kick a ball around, whistle a tune or play the kazoo—to do the things today's adults had time to do when they were growing up.*
>
> —Leslie Dreyfus

The large number of American children who have gone through our schools without mastering the basic skills like reading and math have increased pressure on educators from parents and politicians to teach these skills as early as preschool and toddler programs. While there is deep cause for concern over the problem, the pressures often neglect all that we know about how children learn. Here we examine

- How a high-quality child care program actually prepares and teaches children skills in reading, math, science, music, art, and so much more through their daily play activities
- How formal lessons, appropriate for older children, can be damaging to the learning process in very young children
- How learning in very young children is a natural process of emotional, social, physical, and cognitive development; how, with the help of their teachers, children learn through their pretend games, their interaction with other children, and the enjoyment of their play activities; how play and learning occur simultaneously in all corners of the room in a high-quality child care program
- How children can be encouraged to think and solve problems on their own
- How teachers can work to aid in the learning and development of children with special problems
- Most of all, how the classroom environment makes children comfortable in expressing themselves about their feelings, creating the sense of security that is necessary for children to learn

The child care school setting seemed so perfect. A classroom appropriately decorated with pictures, numbers, and letters of the alphabet. The teacher, a young woman named Sharon, in front of a group of children, about 4 years old, displaying flash cards. The children sitting at small chairs and tables, calling out the letters or numbers on the cards. No noise or chaos. No children walking around the room wasting time. No frills like toys that simply make noise without purpose.

And then, later on, the art project with the teacher preparing the material and instructing the children on how and where to paste or color so that they learn to do it "the right way."

And the worksheets the children take home at the end of the day—*homework*, mind you, for 4-year-olds.

A child care center devoted to one mission. It's day completely planned around what the children needed to be thoroughly prepared for school. A perfect setting. Toddlers calling out letters and numbers. Preschoolers being made ready for the lessons they will be learning in just a year or two as they make the crossover to a regular school setting. Preparing them for the rigors of learning. Giving them a jump start in today's highly competitive world to meet the new challenge of higher standards and making sure every child is learning to read. Meeting the demands of many anxious parents who worry about their children being prepared for school. The setting in Sharon's classroom is the answer to a parent's dream for his preschooler.

Or is it?

Make no mistake about it. All around the country the pressures are mounting. Criticisms of the current state of education are an expected part of every political discussion at both national and local levels. The criticisms are, in many ways, well deserved. The high rate of teenage and adult illiteracy in the world's most advanced industrial nation is shocking. According to a study commissioned by a committee of Congress in 1984, 26 million adults were functionally illiterate, and an additional 49 million did not function proficiently, a total of 72 million Americans who, in terms of literacy, functioned at a marginal level or below.[94] All this has created pressures on educators to ensure that all children learn to read in the early grades.

Now, don't get us wrong. It's certainly an important goal, getting every child to learn to read and do math. The problem is that when pressures like this build up, all that we know about *how* children learn usually goes down faster than the *Titanic*. Teachers, psychologists, social workers, and others who work with children then often find themselves throwing all their years of study of child development into the trash bin as they join in the crush to prepare everyone, from wide-eyed tots to gawking preteens, for the next test in which they will be blackening in pages upon pages of multiple-choice bubbles.

In this atmosphere it's easy to lose sight of the fact that young children learn best when they feel emotionally secure and motivated. For people who work with toddlers and preschoolers, the issue is a crucial one. Parents want their children prepared for school. And getting them ready to learn to read is a very important function of the job of preschool educators. The question is: What's the best way to go about it? Can you just take a group of toddlers or preschoolers, throw them into a classroom situation without any regard for their emotional needs or for the way children learn at that age, and expect to get desirable results?

This is not the first time in our recent history that such a phenomenon has occurred. Back in the late fifties after the Soviet Union launched the first space satellite, *Sputnik*, there was an uproar in our country about how American education was not "keeping up with the Joneskis." Without any new knowledge about child development or education, political and military leaders launched an assault upon the way American children were learning and demanded an all-out approach to teaching cognitive skills, particularly science and math, as far down as the earliest school and preschool grades. One such critic, an admiral in the U.S. Navy, Hyman G. Rickover, made the scornful assertion that while young children in Russia were being trained in science and math, their counterparts in America were busy "finger painting." One prominent early childhood educator, Edward F. Zigler, a professor at Yale University who later became director of Yale's Center in Child Development and Social Policy, was an advocate of the need to nurture all aspects of early development in the child, including the physical, socioemotional, and cognitive systems. He remembers getting an angry call at the time from Admiral Rickover, whom he had never met, castigating him for championing the "whole-child approach" instead of paying primary attention to cognition.[95] Overlooked in this disdainful dismissal of finger painting was how much the young child was actually learning by doing it, everything from color identification to texture to observation of the world around her. And because she still did not have the vocabulary or the skill to speak or write about her feelings and about what she saw in the world, finger painting was a necessary step in developing her communication skills and a building block to speech and writing later on.

"When we recognize the young child's unique modes of learning and adapt educational practices to them, we engage in healthy education," noted Dr. David Elkind, professor of child study and senior resident scholar at Tufts University. "When we ignore what we know about how young children learn and expose them to teaching practices appropriate to children at older age levels, we miseducate them and put them at risk for a sense of inferiority and helplessness."[96]

A child's fascination with a book.

The problem in Sharon's class is that in bending to the pressures of forcing preschool children into "learning readiness," Sharon was doing more harm than good. And so are many of the preschools that are caving in to these pressures of nervous parents and pandering politicians seeking election issues. Introducing a curriculum in preschool that is not suited for them and then forcing children to listen to information and learn letters and numbers will not prepare them for school. It often leads, instead, to undue stress for both the child and the parent and a feeling of inadequacy and a loss of self-esteem for the child. Ultimately, in many children it results in the child's being easily discouraged and developing a dislike for learning.

Well, that was Sharon's class in one child care center. Let's compare it with the practice in a child care center with a different approach to learning.

LEARNING AS A NATURAL PROCESS

Remember Pepper Robinson's toddler class that we saw in Chapter 1? Everything done in the class was actually preparing the children to learn and to succeed in life. But it was not done through formal lessons or academic drill. The basic element of the class was what could be accomplished by the relationship between the teacher and the children—by creating in the toddlers a confidence and emotional warmth in the relationship they had with their teacher they were exploring their universe and being prepared for life.

The same rule applies when the young child becomes a preschooler or a kindergartner. Learning is a continuing process of emotional, social, physical, and cognitive development, each experience building upon the ones before. Zigler and colleagues gave a classroom example of this in their book. "Louis and Philip are sitting in a large box," they wrote. "They are playing 'fishing' and the box has become their 'boat.' They decorated the box with magic markers, using many colors. With their teacher's help, they fashioned a pole, using Legos and a long string attached to one end. The boys 'sail' out to sea and take turns catching the fish. When a storm comes, we hear much giggling and silly noises as their 'boat' begins to rock back and forth. They are playing make-believe. In the course of their play, they cooperate, share, take turns, talk to each other when they disagree, but most of all, they are having fun. Unfortunately, many children do not play as imaginatively as these boys. However, with the help of teachers, parents, or other caregivers, children can learn how to play and, as they engage in their pretend games, develop many of the skills they will need for entry into kindergarten."[97]

Or as Greenspan wrote:

> Unfortunately, the compartmentalization of our post industrial society has tempted many of us into thinking that our minds are similarly compartmentalized. If we want to impart some knowledge, we offer our children facts. If we want to teach loving, we simply say "I love you" or hug. Just as most of us run into a store

T Is for Turkey

Sally, the teacher, is sitting and talking with a girl, Angela.

Sally: What did you do Thanksgiving?

Angela: I went to Shelter Island. I ate pasta.

Sally: No turkey?

Angela: My cousins went with me. I ate turkey.

Sally: What does "turkey" start with? (pronounces the sound of the letter "T" and says the name of the letter. She then writes a sentence describing what the girl did and the girl traces the sentence.)

to purchase a shirt and no longer remember how to grow the flax, pick it, spin it into thread, weave it into linen fabric, and then sew it into a garment, we've forgotten that building a creative, healthy mind in our children isn't a process of one-stop shopping for supercharged "educational" experiences. Just as the linen shirt on your back has its roots in a flax seed planted in the soil, so does your child's personality grow out of the nurturing matrix of interactions with him.

Emotional interactions are also the source of her intelligence, morality, and self-esteem. The loving, intimate connection forged between you and your baby [and, by extension, your young child] sets the stage for your child's higher thinking skills.[98]

In the face of the pressures to teach academics currently being brought on early childhood educators, Rosa Lee Young has remained firm in its commitment to the sound principles of its mission. And sometimes this has not pleased those parents who, succumbing to the current pressures for academic success, want their children to begin formal lessons at the earliest age.

"We had a mother this past school year that really wanted an academic program for her 3-year-old," recalled Director Jeannine Rey. "She wanted paper. She kept asking, 'When are you going to teach him how to write? When are you going to teach him how to read? My friends' children come home from nursery school and they have papers.'

"Well, we're a developmental program. We generate lots of paper. They're not papers the teacher makes up for the children; they're papers the children are doing. They're children's work in a variety of pens and markers and pencils and staplers and tape and hole punchers and whatever they think they need. Some children are writing and some children aren't, but this mother wanted her child to be pushed academically. The mother wanted homework. We have a developmentally appropriate program but the mother kept asking, 'Where's the homework?'

"So we gave the mother a copy of our curriculum. We wanted her to see where the math, the science, the social studies, the language involvement, the reading, the writing comes into this developmental program. But we're not going to give children homework at that young age."

Eventually, the parent's insistence on homework and teacher-generated ditto sheets, the papers that some very young children are bringing home with alphabets and drills, came into conflict with the school's philosophy, and she found another center for her child. "Well, I say that's OK," Jeannine said with a shrug. "She has a right to find that academic, behaviorist program that she wants for her child. There are children who can learn no matter what kind of program you put them in. Will they really develop in all the ways they possibly could? I don't necessarily think so. Some kids will be harmed by that, and some kids don't need our program because it's not structured enough."

But the kids here will be just as academically prepared for school, she insists. And "they will be better prepared in the whole social component in dealing with their world."

A Child and a Butterfly

Let's look at one child at Rosa Lee Young, a 5-year-old boy named Arnold in the prekindergarten class taught by Lisa Streb and Sally Ann Braman. Arnold lives with his mother and stepfather, and visits his biological father frequently. He was an only child for five years until his mother had another child. He seems upset about the new baby. His mother says that she babies him and admits that she has a lot of trouble setting boundaries for him. In class the teachers noted that he enjoys physical activities. When the class goes outdoors, he loves to climb and engage in sports. Indoors, he likes spatial activities—building and creating with blocks. He also likes to write. He writes his name and has begun writing consonants, the easiest letters for a child to understand because they symbolize the sounds made with the lips and tongue. But he is still an angry child, gets discouraged easily, and needs help in his social skills. At times he has gotten so angry that the teacher has advised him to take deep breaths to calm himself down.

Taking a strictly cognitive or academic approach would be difficult enough with all children. It would be especially difficult with Arnold, who, like millions of other American children his age, come into school and child care with special problems of their own. Lisa and Sally's primary job with Arnold is to provide a calm and caring atmosphere for him. They often take him off to a quiet corner to play with him one-on-one. They also take pains to pair him with another child who empathizes with him and provides a calming influence for him. They play games to work on his communications skills because by strengthening his ability to express himself he will be less frustrated and angry.

"Hello! Who's speaking please?"

Too often, children like Arnold are labeled as "learning disabled" or "at risk" or having "attention deficit disorder" or some other name that causes teachers to "minimize or ignore strengths and competencies a child possesses that could promote adaptation and wellness."[99]

As we wrote in Chapter 2, when encouraged, many of these children develop resiliency, an "ability to overcome challenges and frustrations. . . . Teachers have a powerful ability to encourage, motivate, and energize their students if they can identify and help children display their unique islands of competence."[100]

Just one episode will illustrate this. In the classroom the teachers had interested the children in setting up a small house, just a bit bigger than a birdhouse, and in it the children had placed five caterpillars along with leaves for food and other materials to replicate a natural setting. The class followed the instructions in a science kit for young children on how to care for the caterpillars. Each day the children checked on the status of their project, as the teachers counseled children to be patient because, as we all know, children are impatient, but nature can't be rushed. And then one day, a day on which I fortunately visited the class, the teacher opened the door and, behold, the caterpillars had turned into five beautiful butterflies. Then they all went out into the playground together to release the butterflies and let them "fly to freedom." Encouraged by the teacher who held their arms one by one, the children put their fingers out in the entrance door to see if each butterfly would perch before flying away. But the butterflies all had other ideas as one by one, they simply fluttered out the door and flew away to the squeals of delight of the junior scientists.

Until the last butterfly. Now it was Arnold's turn. As his eyes opened wide as saucers, he watched breathlessly as the butterfly made its way to the door and, then, suddenly fluttered a bit and perched on his index finger. The child was beside himself with joy as the teacher slowly showed him how to move his hand and send the butterfly out into the world "to freedom." The expression on his face told it all. What an accomplishment for this child!

And what an experience for the class. Afterward, the teachers encouraged the children to describe what they had seen and then draw it. This wonderful fun project, this game they played, without ditto sheets or note cards or drills or having to "learn" anything. But, oh, what they did learn from it. They learned science, the process that we call metamorphosis in nature that turns a larva into an adult insect. They learned communications skills by using language to describe what they saw. They learned to recall their visions by drawing them. They developed the concept of symmetry as they drew the wings on each side of the bodies. They took steps down the path toward reading as they read stories and poems about butterflies. They strengthened their fine motor skills by fashioning playdough into caterpillars and butterflies. They engaged in music and movement activities as they used their imaginations to become dancing butterflies. They reinforced their knowledge of days, dates, and numbers by keeping track on their class calendar of the number of days it took to hatch the butterflies. They even had a Spanish vocabulary lesson, learning words like *oriega* (caterpillar) and *mariposa* (butterfly). By cooperating with each other on the project, they learned to work closely with their peers. And, finally, they learned to respect life and nature by setting the butterflies free. What an experience! And not a teacher-generated ditto sheet in sight.

PLAY IS THE WORK OF THE CHILD

Given that one of the principal functions of a good early child care program is to prepare children for school, the question we have to ask is: "What's the best way for them to do this?" Or more specifically in this case: "How does Rosa Lee Young do it and is it successful?"

As we have seen, preparation for school is by no means only setting the stage for learning to read or write or add or subtract. School casts the child into a social situation with adults and with peers. School preparedness must include the ability of the child to share, to cooperate with others in his class, to listen to instructions, to express himself creatively, and to get self-satisfaction from his accomplishments—the emotional and social side of his development. "Adherents of the whole child approach do not devalue the importance of cognitive skills, including literacy," emphasized Zigler. "No reasonable person would argue against the merits of literacy. . . . However, reading is only one

Hopping, Hugging, and Learning

The nine children in the prekindergarten and kindergarten class of Sally Braman and Jessica Venetucci are going through their morning greetings at circle time (three are absent this day). Even a cursory look reveals that the entire proceedings are at once a physical exercise, a chance for fun, and an opportunity to learn. The children have already learned to raise their hands and be recognized by the teacher, an important part of the socialization process that prepares them for school.

Sally asks children what day is today as she points to the date on a large calendar. Children raise hands. Sally calls on one child.

Child (reads date): November 26, 2007.

Sally (turning a large weather wheel to indicate the day's weather): What's the weather today?

(Children raise hands.)

Child reads: Raining.

Sally (pointing to a chart with the number 57 on it): How many days in school?

(Children raise hands.)

Child reads: Fifty-seven.

Sally (holding up a jar containing beans and again pointing to the number on the chart): How many beans in this jar?

(Children raise hands.)

Child: Fifty-seven.

Sally: Let's see. Shall we count them?

(She pours out the beans into a bowl and leads them as they all count together, 1-2-3-4 . . . until they get to 56, the last one).

Sally: Oh, we need to add one for today. Fifty-six and one more (as she adds another bean) makes . . .

(She points to the chart. Some children call out, others raise hands. Sally calls on one with a hand raised.)

Child: Fifty-seven

Sally (holding up a box containing small sticks and again pointing to the number on the chart): How many sticks in this box?

(Children raise hands, and the same sequence is repeated, this time with sticks in the box.)

Child: I got a boo-boo.

Sally: OK, tell me about it later. We'll take care of it. (To class): Who can count by 10 to 100.

(A child raises her hand.)

(Continued)

Continued

Child (as Sally claps to each number): 10, 20, 30, 40, 50, 60, 70, 80, 90, 100.

Sally: Now, let's all do it.

(She repeats the process and the entire class counts the same way.)

(At this point, another child, Loren, who is holding a doll belonging to her, comes in with her father.)

Sally: Let's make a circle and hop to the days of the week. (She leads the children in a circle and they all hop as Sally recites): Sunday, Monday, Tuesday, Wednesday, Thursday, Friday, Saturday. (To Loren): Loren, could you put your baby in the cubby? (Loren does it.) Now could you give me a hug? (Loren hugs Sally.)

(Meanwhile, Loren's dad remains. It's hard for him to part. He stays, hugging and kissing his daughter, until the child finally puts her hand out and turns away, signaling, "Enough, leave already." Dad gets the message and departs only after he hugs and kisses his daughter one more time.)

aspect of cognitive development, and cognitive development is only one aspect of human development. Cognitive skills are very important but they are so intertwined with the physical, social, and emotional systems that it is myopic, if not futile, to dwell on the intellect and exclude its partners."[101]

School Success Means the Three Rs . . . and Much More

Elaborating on this further, Zigler wrote, "Consider what goes into literacy. It involves mastery of the alphabet, phonemes, and other basic word skills, for certain." But children who have physical or emotional problems will have difficulty learning to read. And by the same token, "a child who begins kindergarten knowing letters and sounds may be cognitively prepared, but if he or she does not understand how to listen, share, take turns, and get along with teachers and classmates, this lack of socialization will hinder further learning. To succeed in reading and at school, a child must receive appropriate education, of course, but he or she must also be physically and mentally healthy, have reasonable social skills, and have curiosity, confidence, and motivation to succeed. This broader view was endorsed in the authoritative book *From Neurons to Neighborhoods* in which the finest child development thinkers in the nation pointed out the importance of emotional and motivational factors in human development and learning."[102]

More specifically, in a chapter written for the *Handbook of Infant Mental Health*, a publication of the World Association for Infant Mental Health, Rebecca Shahmoon Shanok, director of the Institute for Infants, Children and Families of the Jewish Board of Family and Children Services, noted that being success-ful in school involves both the social and the learning-cognitive areas of the child's development and that each one is fundamental to both early, intermedi-ate, and long-term success. Quoting from a paper published by Zero to Three, she listed those qualities that make for success in both areas:

1. *Confidence*—A sense of control and mastery of one's body, behavior and world, the child's sense that he is more likely than not to succeed at what he undertakes, and that adults will be helpful.

2. *Curiosity*—The sense that finding out about things is positive and leads to pleasure.

3. *Intentionality*—The wish and capacity to have an impact, and to act with persistence. This is clearly related to a sense of competence, of being effective.

4. *Self-control*—The ability to modulate and control one's own actions in age-appropriate ways; a sense of inner control.

5. *Relatedness*—The ability to engage with others based on the sense of being understood by and understanding others.

6. *Capacity to Communicate*—The wish and ability to verbally exchange ideas, feelings, and concepts to others. This is related to a sense of trust in others and of pleasure in engaging with others, including adults.

7. *Cooperativeness*—The ability to balance one's own needs with those of others in a group activity.[103]

Above all, the emphasis in all good child care and preschool programs must be *play*. Play is the work of the child. It is the way she accomplishes her daily tasks. In a good preschool program, play will lead to curiosity and experiences that sharpen the child's natural desire to learn more about the world around her. The teacher follows the lead of the child and uses the child's curiosity to pave the way for the more formal learning that develops as she advances in ele-mentary school grades. A good program prepares the child to cooperate with teachers and peers, gives her confidence, and builds her social skills. She learns how to regulate herself, to control her anger in ways that are socially beneficial. In short, it builds in her the social, emotional, and intellectual skills necessary for later success in school.

A good summary of the role of play in preschool learning was contained in a 2003 article in *Young Children*, the Journal of the National Association for the Education of Young Children. Citing studies focusing on the relationship between play and literacy, the authors concluded that when young children engaged in a program of play in child care, it "resulted in an increase in the children's use of literacy materials and their engagement in literary acts, as well as gains in specific literacy skills. . . . Not only does play help children develop skills and concepts necessary to master literacy and math, it also builds the foundation of more general competencies that are necessary for children to learn successfully in school and beyond." They also drew on their own work with preschool, Head Start, and kindergarten classes to support their finding that high-level play (i.e., play that has some degree of a plan the children and teachers create in which they can describe to each other what the scheme is and who is playing which specific role) "has a positive effect on the development of foundational skills, including cognitive and emotional self-regulation and the ability to use symbols. These foundational skills in turn make it possible for children to achieve high levels of mastery of specific academic content, such as literacy."[104]

Children do this, the authors noted, citing the earlier pioneering works of Lev Vygotsky and his student, Daniel Elkonin, when they engage in *mature play*, which include four steps that are necessary for the child to profit from academic activities. Mature play

1. Affects the child's motivation to achieve immediate and long-term goals and teaches the child for the first time to delay gratification, a difficult task for preschoolers but one that is necessary to achieve success in learning
2. Allows the child to take into account the perspectives in other people as he must coordinate his own needs with the needs of others. In doing so, he must negotiate play scenarios and coordinate his perspectives with those of his peers and his teachers, a necessary step toward reflective thinking.
3. Moves him to substitute replicas for real objects (a doll represents a person, a box is a house, a wooden block is a car, etc.), which leads to his substitution of new objects that look different but perform the same function. Eventually, he doesn't need the object but simply uses images and symbolic substitutes in his speech, the beginning of the development of abstract thinking.
4. Teaches him to follow rules, organize activities in successive order, first in physical activities and later in mental processes such as memory, problem solving, and attention to a task

They concluded, "Our research shows that an emphasis on play does not detract from academic learning but actually enables children to learn." In classrooms where children spent a substantial portion of the day in play that followed the principles outlined above, "children scored higher in literacy skills than in control classrooms." "Play," they emphasized, "does not compete with foundational skills: Through mature play, children learn the very foundational skills that will prepare them for the academic challenges that lie ahead."[105]

Let's look now at how some of the specific qualities that make for success in school have been applied to the children at Rosa Lee Young.

As we have seen, 4- and 5-year-olds who have been at the center since they entered as toddlers have actually been preparing for several years. In effect, from the time they first entered its doors, *they have been learning how to learn.* They have been listening to stories, drawing and constructing, having their imaginations challenged and stimulated, learning how to cooperate with their peers and adults on interesting projects, communicating their ideas and feelings to others, and discovering the wonders of the world around them through all their play activities. Most important, they have been encouraged to explore and create on their own. They have also come to understand that the stories that have been read to them, the ideas they have expressed, and the pictures they have drawn bear a unique relationship to those curious markings on a printed page called letters, words, and sentences, and many have already started to recognize words, the first big step toward reading.

We can best see how this works out concretely by sitting in on a class at the Rosa Lee Young center, the prekindergarten and kindergarten class taught by Lisa Streb and Sally Ann Braman. There are twelve 4- and 5-year-old children in the class. On the day I visited, eleven of them were present. Most of them have been there for several years and, therefore, can be said to be the product of Rosa Lee Young training since they were toddlers. They will all be going into first grade in the public schools in one or two years. Will they be ready for reading and math? Will they be ready to participate in the social situation of a public school? More to the point, will they be better or worse off for the fact that they were not trained in formal lessons with ditto sheets and flash cards? Let's go into the class and watch how it functions.

There is a distinct informality in many ways to classes at the school. Although punctuality is a desirable asset taught in most classroom settings, it is recognized that the children's parents are working people who leave for work at different times and drop their children off accordingly. So, beginning at 8 a.m., the children begin to trickle in and are welcomed individually, and no one makes a fuss over the different times the children arrive. By 9:30 all the children are usually there. The teachers work with the children present, and as more arrive they are greeted and quickly integrated into the proceedings. The morning I visited the pre-K and kindergarten class was no exception. By the time all the children had arrived, the class was a veritable beehive of varied activity. There were five distinct activities going on at the same time but all carefully supervised by the two teachers in charge. In one area of the room, three children were at the crafts table drawing and painting with water colors. They were all busily engrossed in the work they were producing—one of them, a tall, round-faced girl named Karen, produced a drawing with patterns of flowers, sun, and a garden. Each child was encouraged by Lisa to talk about her drawing. As each one finished her drawing, it was hung on display from the clothesline strung for that purpose across the back of the classroom. Lisa walked around to each group in turn making sure that she engaged every child in the classroom individually.

In another area four children were absorbed at two computers, two at each one, playing an educational video game. They were excited, and each pair talked animatedly between themselves about the game in which they were engaged. Further down the room, two children gave each other instructions as they dished out sand in cups and bowls in the family corner, pretending they were preparing and eating food. And across the room three others were sponge painting, dabbing patterns of color on paper with small kitchen sponges. And all the while Lisa moved from group to group, talking to the children, giving them directions without appearing to dominate them, encouraging them, helping to solve their problems as they arose. The children were free to move from one area to the other, but Lisa was always there with a gentle word to make sure they didn't just jump from one activity to another but stayed at one place long enough to accomplish a significant task.

Writing a Class Story

As all this was going on, Sally sat at a table in another area of the room and called up one child at a time. Together, Sally and each child wrote a story about an experience the class had the day before—a trip to a store in town that is a natural for utilization by teachers of young children eager to provide their charges with enriching experiences.

Parrot World is a unique little retail establishment on Sunrise Highway, one of Long Island's main arteries, in the heart of Rockville Centre. It is a pet shop that sells many different animals but specializes in parrots and other exotic birds. A day earlier the children visited the shop, and now they were going to use the tools they were learning to tell the world about it.

Each child in turn came to the table and sat down next to Sally and, responding to questions, told her what she saw at Parrot World. The questions

" 'R' is for red."

she asked were designed to move the story along in the child's mind and get her to think and speak in a logical sequence. "And what happened next?" "And what did you see after that?" As they spoke Sally printed meticulously what they said. Some children spoke longer than others, and some expressed themselves in only two or three sentences—it didn't matter. Under Sally's questioning, a story emerged from each child's mind as a sequential order of events. Then each child drew a picture of what she had described in words. Next to the picture, Sally then displayed the words the children had used to describe their experience, reading the words back and pointing to each word, demonstrating naturally how words are used to express the things we see and how each story they told had a beginning, a middle, and an end, the way stories and books are made. Then each child proudly wrote her name under the story she had told and the picture she had drawn (by then each could print her name and some could even print some common words) and the collection of stories and pictures made up a book the class wrote. When it was finished, it went up on display, a true *magnum opus* of the class. *War and Peace* could hardly have been more of a literary accomplishment—relatively speaking, of course.

You could see signs of the way the children were learning about words and numbers all around the classroom. A child at the drawing table who had drawn something and wanted to write the word for it, asking the teacher how to spell it and then tracing or writing the letters. Children in the family corner counting out the number of bowls they needed for the table. All done in a very natural way as part of their everyday activities. *But in no sense haphazardly because the school, as we have seen, has a curriculum that teachers follow and to which the activities are tailored. This curriculum is adapted and modified by each teacher based upon the interests that develop among the children in her class.*

THE LEARNING CENTERS

Essential to the Rosa Lee Young curriculum are the clearly defined learning centers that are organized in each of the toddler, pre-K, and kindergarten classrooms. These learning centers evolve; materials are changed and added to accommodate new steps in the children's learning patterns and various current themes and subjects of interest (holidays, seasons, etc.) throughout the year. Materials and equipment selected for these centers foster creativity, exploration, and inquiry. Learning centers are accessible for children; are bright, attractive, and inviting; foster active engagement; are clearly defined and labeled; and are equipped with age-appropriate materials that are integrated within the daily routine and curriculum plans.

Here is a list of learning centers and materials and props used in them. (*For a more comprehensive picture of the part these centers and materials play in the work done with the children at the school, see the school's curriculum, reprinted in Appendix A.*)

Library: books, magazines, posters, puppets, photos, flannel board

Listening: cassette/compact disk player, head phones, books with audio

Dramatic play: authentic props (clothing, hats, career-related tools), print materials (books, magazines, other materials) that help children act out male and female adult roles in a variety of settings

Blocks: unit blocks with complementary accessories such as mathematical patterns, figurines of animals and people, small toys

Music: rhythm instruments, instrumental and choral music

Math/manipulative: picture puzzles, simple board games, table blocks, Unifix cubes, tangrams, Legos, beads for stringing, standard and non-standard measuring tools, Cuisenaire rods

Writing: lined and unlined paper of various sizes, large pencils, markers, crayons, print stamps, computers

Science: plants, dirt, rocks, seeds, leaves, flowers, magnifiers, measuring tools, classroom pets

Sand and water play: plastic containers of various sizes and shapes

Creative arts: easels, playdough, paint, sand, water, glue sticks, paste, scissors, tape, paper of different sizes, colors, and textures

Large muscle: riding toys, jump ropes, hula hoops, balls, indoor and outdoor equipment for activities such as climbing and sliding

The use of these learning tools and other learning experiences is written into the overall schedule at the school. The schedule provides that every morning, after 9:30 when all the children are there and they have been welcomed as a group at circle time, four definite blocks of time are planned for the rest of the morning.

THE DAILY SCHEDULE

The first block is called *planning time* in which the children are divided into two smaller groups, each with a teacher, and they plan what they will do during *work/play* time that follows. Children choose what activity they would like. In the toddler class, the choices are usually limited to three—Pepper, remember, gave them the choice of the doll corner, the reading area (where they pasted figures from *The Three Bears* on the flannel board), and the water table. In classes of the older children, the choices are greater because their range of experience is greater. They can go to one of the learning centers listed earlier. The teacher encourages them to express what they want to do at the center, what game they want to play, what they want to draw, or what book they want to read. If too many children choose any one activity, the teacher gently persuades one or two to change his mind with a promise that he'll get his chance when one of the others grows tired and switches. That usually is enough to persuade a child to temporarily seek another area of activity.

After the planning the children spend time at the *learning areas*, working as planned with teachers moving among them, observing, recording, interacting, and expanding on the activities of the children. All the areas are open to the children and they often switch areas when they grow tired of one particular activity.

As they work, and immediately afterward, they are encouraged to *recall* what they have done by discussing with the teachers how they have accomplished what they set out to do. They are usually then encouraged to express themselves about what they did by writing it, drawing it, or constructing it with blocks or clay, or using music, dramatic play, or movement to illustrate it.

Finally, there are *teacher directed activities* that are specifically designed and planned to give children experiences with different concepts and materials. The materials are chosen in advance in accord with an overall plan that is designed to allow the teacher to deal with an area of common interest to the children and with the aim of developing specific skills and getting them to know specific information.

As we said it's all play, but it's all work and learning too. Let's see how it operates in another class, the prekindergarten class taught by Jeannine Hogan and Janet Matthews, and how the learning that takes place using the school's techniques really prepares the children for learning the rest of their lives.

The class is composed of eleven 3- and 4-year-olds. It is one of two classes at the school for children in this age group. When I arrived at the class at about 8:30 a.m., most were already there and were busy with morning activities as parents arrived to drop off their children. Four children were busy in the block area; some were off in another area playing with Legos. One child was in the reading area, reading a picture book to herself. The teachers' voices were soft and direct, and always respectful. Soon it came time to put the blocks away and come together as a class. Janet made it a game. "I spy a block over here" or "I spy a block over there," she would say, and children would get each one and return it to its proper place of storage. It didn't always go smoothly. Sometimes a child was distracted into something else or just didn't feel like picking up the blocks, but Janet always showed patience, and a gentle reminder that we all have to clean up after ourselves was usually all that was needed to get them back to the task at hand. The result was a big note of accomplishment for children of this age because when the blocks were all put away and the teacher complimented them, they all looked proud of what they had done.

In referring to a child's classmate, both teachers consistently used the word *friend*. "Please help your friend find the other block" or "Please help your friend put that toy away." One of the basic aims of all classes at the school is to get the children to treat each other with respect. This applied also when a child suddenly would not interact well with others and would disrupt their play. A very interesting thing to note as I watched the class was the nonjudgmental behavior of the teachers toward each child. When a dispute inevitably arose between two children, the teacher would not judge or blame either one but would hold them both around and get them to talk about what happened, encouraging them to seek ways to settle the problem.

When the class was gathered, Jeannine asked the children if they would like to hear her read a book one of the children had chosen. They agreed. It was called *Alligator Under My Bed*. As she read the children interrupted with comments, sometimes about the story, often with their imaginations running far afield. "I have an alligator under my bed," said one. Not to be outdone, another revealed, "I have a monster under my bed."

"What kind of a monster?" asked the teacher.

"A big one," he answered.

"And where did he go," she wanted to know.

The little boy shrugged a bit to signify that he did not know.

The reading continued in this way, with the story a vehicle to stir the imagination of the children and get them to think and associate the book with a life experience, real or imaginary.

The children all showed interest in the book, often standing up to come closer to Jeannine as she read, so that she sometimes had to remind them to "sit on their bottoms" so that children sitting behind them could see. As could be expected with children of this age, the reading was not without complications. When one child spoke excitedly about the story, another complained that she talked "too loud." Another claimed that the child next to her was "too close to her body." In each case, the teacher's reaction was sympathetic. "I know it's too loud for you; we'll try to lower our voices a bit" or "Tell Derek that he's too close to your body, and I'm sure he'll move away a bit; isn't that so, Derek?" After the alligator story, she read another book chosen by Charles about workers putting up buildings. She stopped during the reading to ask the children questions about the story.

"Who are the people wearing yellow hats?" she queried.

"Construction workers," Charles answered.

"Your daddy is a construction worker, isn't he?" asked the teacher. Charles nodded.

"And what does he do?"

"He makes houses."

Referring to the story, she then asked, "What are they doing?"

"Making a house," several children chorused.

After reading the book, it was 9:30, circle time, and all the children gathered around for a "hello" song. Then it was time for a special song, and Jeannine asked if anyone had a favorite he wanted them all to sing. Charles responded with "If I Had a Hammer," and Jeannine knitted her brow and asked, "How did I know you were going to want to sing that song?" Being a successful teacher of young children often involves being an inspired actor, and Jeannine was no exception. So they all sang,

> *If I had a hammer,*
>
> *I'd hammer in the morning,*
>
> *I'd hammer in the evening,*
>
> *All over this land. . . .*

As they sang, following the lead of the teacher, they acted out the song, making hammering motions with their hands.

Circle time is observed in many child care situations—the time when all the children come together. At Rosa Lee Young each teacher handles circle time differently. At times, when a child found it difficult to sit with the group during circle time, a teacher played with the child in a different area of the room.

Children at this age express their anxieties in a number of ways. As Jeannine and Janet greeted the children with a "How are you today?" one child answered, "My mommy's sick."

Jeannine, who had spoken with the child's mother just an hour earlier, responded, "I talked with your mommy today, and she's just going to the dentist. She will be all better. And how are you today?"

As the children sat in a circle, she asked each one what they liked and drew the things they said on a card for each of them. She said they would be the *symbols* for each child, explained what a symbol was, and then carefully lettered the child's name on the card above his symbol. One child was a yellow sun, another was a red heart, and so on. One child asked Jeannine, "What is your symbol?"

"Well, I like fishing and riding horses," she said. "So my symbol should be a fish and a horseshoe.

With story time and circle time over, they headed for the playground outside. That meant putting on coats, a process in which each child needed the teacher's help. It was done calmly and efficiently, and as the children were finished, they sat on the floor waiting for the others. When they were all ready, they lined up at the teacher's instruction. One of the children, a girl named Karen, began to cry because she wanted to stand behind Christina and another child was there first. The teachers calmed her and when she then expressed her wishes verbally instead of crying, Jeannine complimented her by saying, "Those are nice words." Karen then calmed down and accepted her place in line. (At a subsequent staff meeting, the teachers reflected upon the fact that children became impatient waiting to go outdoors as a single group while the teachers helped each child put on their coats. It was decided that in the future, the classes would be divided into two groups with one teacher taking the first half of the class out as soon as they were ready, rather than have them wait for the rest to get dressed.)

During playground time I noticed that Christina, who had come to the United States from South America just twelve weeks earlier and spoke only Spanish when she arrived, was now exhibiting a proficiency in many English words. She began to pat pieces of soil together, playing at cooking some South American dishes. She then came over and offered them to me. I pretended to take them and eat them, and I suggested that she offer them to a friend. Charles happened to be standing nearby, and she turned to him and offered him her pretend food. They both played at this game for a while.

They were just about ready to go back to the class when Karen provoked Christina by grabbing away her sand bucket. Christina grabbed it back and Karen began to cry. Janet held both children around and listened to their complaints, settling them down. When they went back upstairs, Janet held Karen's hand.

"This book looks interesting. Let's see what's inside."

It was obvious in every situation that the teachers knew the personalities of the children and were quick to anticipate any conflict or crisis before it happened. When they spotted a troublesome situation arising, they would often try to discuss it with the children involved before it progressed to the crisis stage. They were gentle with the children and allowed them a great deal of choice in activities, but they knew how to enforce rules that were there for the common benefit of all the children and for their safety. In the playground, for example, Philip and Charles climbed on top of a plastic tunnel together. Karen came along and wanted to climb up too. The teachers decided that it was not safe for the children to be sitting on top of the tunnel, and that they all had to come down. The boys weren't too pleased with the teachers' decision, but they came down anyway.

Planning for the Unforeseen

When they were back in the classroom, Jeannine asked the children if they would like to join her at the drawing table to make cards for their mothers because Mother's Day was approaching. She worked with one child at a time while the others played at the various areas of the room—the family corner, the doll house, the Legos area.

Suddenly, in the middle of all the activity, Ralph began to cry and looked as if he was going to throw up. He did. But assisted by Janet, he made it to the bathroom just in time. Jeannine had to stop her work with the children at the drawing table to go out and call Ralph's mother to arrange to take him home. She explained to the children that she had to stop working with them so she could call Ralph's mother because Ralph wasn't feeling well. They went to other activities, supervised by Janet as Jeannine left with Ralph to make her call. But as circumstances would have it, this was just the moment that Jeannine's daughter, a child in the toddler class at the school, also chose to get sick and throw up. It was not an epidemic, but it was quite a coincidence. The office then took over. Jeannine Rey and social worker Barbara Andrzejewski stopped what they were doing, phoned Ralph's mother, and then made arrangements to have Christine Healy substitute for Jeannine Hogan, who had to take her daughter to the doctor. Christine is a teacher who works with children in the after-school program. These children come to Rosa Lee Young after their regular school day is over until their working parents pick them up later in the afternoon. During the morning and early afternoon, Christine acts as a *floater*, a teacher who fills in for teachers on their breaks or when a teacher has to leave in an emergency. She is a permanent member of the staff, and all the children know her, so there is no problem with small children getting used to a stranger. Child care centers must always plan for such contingencies.

All through the day, in this and in other classes at Rosa Lee Young, the same goals and methods apply in working with children. Teachers are always involved with them, whether they are together as a whole class or playing in separate areas. They consistently interact with the children as part of their play scene. They encourage the children to play with their peers in a respectful manner. When a conflict arises, the children are encouraged to try to resolve it by talking and negotiating with each other, but they know that if they can't, the teachers are there to help them. They often calm a child down by telling her to take a deep breath because it usually helps the child feel a little better and it takes time away from the conflict.

Most significant, when a child's behavior is not appropriate, the teacher still doesn't treat him with disrespect. She talks to him. She talks about what behavior was appropriate. She encourages him to use words to negotiate conflicts or to express what he was feeling.

But when a child is too distressed to talk, the teacher comforts her to calm her down. Speaking this way to a child in a calm voice is far more effective in changing undesirable behavior at that age than the so-called punishments often meted out to such young children, who hardly know what they are being punished for. I contrasted this in my mind with an earlier experience at a child care center where a big chair was reserved against a wall for children who were given time-outs. If a child transgressed, it was a time-out for him, and he was put in the chair, often having to be carried kicking and screaming to his punishment. And he usually sat there, crying hysterically until the teacher got ready to let him come back. He never had any real understanding of what his "crime" was and, therefore, frequently repeated the behavior. This was called *discipline*. The fact that it led to much more hostility among the children, far more anxiety, and far more classroom problems didn't seem to matter. Punishment was punishment. What a pleasure not to see children handled in this way. And what a difference in the results.

ALL THE THINGS THEY WERE LEARNING

I said earlier that this class did far more to prepare children for reading than all the formal lessons, flash cards, and ditto sheets that some child care programs were going in for. Let's now take a look back and see how this class, *where the children were seemingly just having fun at play for the entire day was actually preparing all of them for school and for learning how to read.*

Let's start with the building of those skills that are specific to cognitive development. As we have seen, children learn to read when they begin to understand the connection between the interesting things they see and the stories they hear and the words on the printed page. The children at Rosa Lee Young have been listening to stories that interest them and drawing and constructing from their experience. In this class the teachers further built upon the development of these skills in a number of ways.

1. When the class gathered around for story time, the children chose a book that they knew from previous readings and that they liked. As the teacher read *Alligator Under My Bed*, the children commented and engaged in dialogue about the story, establishing a connection between their thoughts and the words the teacher was reading from the book. When the teacher read another book, selected by Charles, about construction workers building a house, it was also familiar to them. They knew what was coming next. The song they sang afterward associated a hammer with building, translating the story into action they could concretely see as their own.

2. The teacher didn't just read the story, she asked questions about it that got them to think. "Who wears yellow hats?" The children's answer, "Construction workers," was the beginning of establishing an understanding in the minds of 3-year-olds that the book is telling us something, a fact that they could see in the pictures and in the concept of people in yellow hats building a house.

3. When they played in the learning areas, they were encouraged to do things on their own, choosing the area of interest to them. Invariably, all the children would spend some time in the reading corner, looking at books on their own, examining the pictures, and remembering the story. The teacher often came along and explained the book and pointed to the words under the pictures so that gradually the child saw the connection between the letters and words and the pictures and story.

4. Similarly, children played on their own with Legos, constructing buildings and towers and experimenting with physical and scientific principles—how high can it go before it unbalances and falls, what makes one piece fit inside another. Keeping track of the Legos and blocks, often with the help of the teacher who counts them as they are used or put away, helps the child to learn the significance of numbers and how to count.

5. When it came time to clean up blocks and toys, the teacher made a game out of it. "I spy a block near the chair" sharpens the children's alertness to the things around them.

6. When Jeannine Hogan lettered each child's name on a card and drew a symbol the child liked and pictured as himself, she used the word *symbol* to signify it. When a child asked her what her symbol was, she told him that she liked fishing and riding horses and, therefore, her symbol should be a fish and a horseshoe. The children not only learned the word *symbol* and what it means but also were able to picture a symbolic object in their minds, helping to build their imaginations.

7. There is a rug map in one area of the room with pictures of roads, bridges, and tunnels over which they drive toy cars. It is a game that gets them to discern directions and read simple diagrams. Children playing in this area often discuss among themselves how to get from one place to another on the map's road and then move the cars to these places.

These and many other activities in the classes build the children's cognitive abilities. But, as so many have pointed out, success in school involves more than just cognitive development. It also involves the development of the child as a social being capable of functioning in a group, of participating in a give and take, of negotiating differences with other children, of following directions from the teacher, of learning to control his raw emotions, and of learning the difference between acceptable and unacceptable social behavior. Let's recount how some of the activities in Jeannine and Janet's class helped to accomplish these goals.

1. First, the accent was always on cooperation and friendship among children playing together. "Help your friend" were not just words. Spoken in a friendly manner that let the children know the teacher was their friend too, it taught the children what the words mean and encouraged a feeling of closeness among the children.

2. The teachers were constantly teaching the children how to settle disputes by negotiation and talking rather than by striking out. When a child complained that another child had come too close or had spoken too loudly or had "touched his body," the first advice of the teacher was, "Tell him not to touch your body" or "Tell him not to come so close." Usually that was enough to get the child in question to back off. If it didn't succeed, the teacher intervened and negotiated a solution. When Karen and Christina were involved in grabbing the bucket from each other, the teacher took them both around and lovingly aided the negotiating process.

3. Children felt confident in telling the teacher what was troubling them. Even if it sometimes was an exaggeration, they were able to express their fears openly. The child who said "My mommy's sick," even though it was only a dental appointment the parent was keeping was expressing something that frightened her. By talking about it and helping to alleviate the fear, the teacher was preventing the child from acting on her fear in another way that might not have been desirable. This was all part of the conscious effort by teachers to have children express their feelings and emotions. Children after the age of 3 or 4 who can do this are far less likely to have tantrums or lash out with hostility toward others.

4. The diverse cultures and languages of the children were respected. Christina, the little girl who served me play South American food from the soil in the playground, often talks in class about dishes that she eats at home. When she came to the class and knew no English, there was a woman who spoke fluent Spanish available, a volunteer we mentioned earlier in the book named Maria Del Valle, whom they all call "Grandma." She helped Christina tremendously to adjust to her new situation, often translating between the children and between the child and the teacher. After just twelve weeks, Christina spoke a great deal of English and was on her way to becoming truly bilingual.

5. The children learned rules by which a social group has to abide. When the children in the playground climbed to the top of the tunnel, the teacher reminded them that this was not safe, and they understood that they had to come down.

6. The incident in which a child threw up was handled very sympathetically, encouraging the same feeling among the children toward a classmate in trouble.

7. Finally, the way the teachers worked with a more difficult child, Karen, was a lesson in the way it should be done. Discipline was used as a learning tool and done lovingly, making it clear that it was not the child who was being criticized but what he did. "Take a deep breath" often helped to forestall anger, and negotiation and compromise was the rule of the day. I contrast this often with some other child care programs that used harsh forms of discipline. In one center, a child who had difficulty speaking was told that unless she said something, she would not get her snack with the other children. Of course, it didn't work, but such a device should never be used in any situation. Threatening to deny children food is something that is highly traumatic to them and is a form of mental abuse. What a difference in this center!

Ann Chin "just happened to stumble" upon the school. She and her husband bought their house in Rockville Centre nearly thirty years ago and "were looking desperately for a child care center." Both were teachers. They had a 3-year-old son, Robert, and like many young parents in the seventies and eighties and most young parents today, the combined incomes of both were needed to pay for the home they were buying for their family. With both parents working, child care was an absolute necessity.

Robert had a private person caring for him for two months, and the experience, according to Ann was "horrendous." They had looked into child care facilities in nearby towns and did not like them. Finally, nearing the point of desperation, they were driving past the old Rosa Lee Young facility in its second church location one day when they noticed a lot of young children playing in the sandyard outside the building. "My husband said to me, 'Why don't we go and see. Maybe this is a day care center. If it isn't, they might know of one.' So we stopped and went in and lo and behold, it was. And that's when I met Joan and saw the center for the first time."

Certain things impressed her right from the beginning. "There was the hubbub of a busy place," she recalled. The kids all seemed to be happy and although there was alert adult supervision, "there was plenty of freedom of movement" for them.

She enrolled Robert, and as time passed she acquired a deep and profound respect for the center's philosophy and its application to the daily work it did with children. "They understood a child's thinking. They didn't pooh-pooh it away. They met Robert's needs at the time, and I was very impressed because Robert was a tough cookie in terms of separation. They understood this and made for the allowance of separation." They also understood that working parents needed some flexibility and they made some special provisions for them. "We had to leave for work by 7:15 and the center didn't open until 7:30, but they made the allowance for us. They opened the school fifteen minutes earlier just for my son. He was the first one in."

And as far as the separation anxiety, that soon tapered off, and Robert became very calm when he was dropped off. "But that was the center's doing," Ann emphasized. "They understood what separation was like. They understood that this was a terrible time for him." And Robert soon came to love the place. "By midyear," she recalled with a bit of a laugh, when she came to pick him up in the afternoon, "I couldn't drag him off the schoolyard. I knew he was happy because I couldn't get him home."

Five years later, after Robert had gone on to public elementary school, her younger son James, born since, was also enrolled. And some years after that, Ann, now a complete devotee of Rosa Lee Young, joined its board of directors.

But it wasn't just that her children were happy at Rosa Lee Young that has made her such an enthusiastic supporter. Whenever she was in the building, she took time to look around at some of the classes, a practice that is encouraged by the school for its parents. What she could see very clearly was that through the play, "there was real learning going on. But it was relaxed. There was no feeling of pressure."

At the time of this writing, Robert was 27. A major in biology while in college, he holds a master's degree in kinesiology, has worked as a recreation director in a large community center, and went on to become a teacher. James graduated from college, majoring in English. Ann Chin gives Rosa Lee Young credit in large measure for getting them off to the right start academically.

Your attitude toward learning and school is established in the early years, she holds. She has known children in her career as a junior high school teacher whose feelings about school were shaped negatively very early on, who never could enjoy school because they were so miserable the first couple of years.

She concedes that when her children went on to public elementary school "it was a bit difficult at first for them to adjust to some things there. The philosophy of teaching here at the center as opposed to elementary school was different. They were both used to having more mobility, and suddenly they were told they had to sit for long periods. It took some getting used to." But they were able to because they had developed in important ways during their early years at Rosa Lee Young. "They had socialization skills. They knew how to share things. They were cooperative with their teachers. They had respect for learning and respect for their teachers and I think that this had a lot to do with the center."

They succeeded, she asserts, because "Rosa Lee Young gave them confidence in themselves."

Does Your Program Encourage Learning That Is Age-Appropriate For Early Childhood?

1. Does the child care program engage in formal lessons, drills, work sheets, and other such forms, or are the children encouraged to learn through hands-on experiences, games, and play?
2. Does the program arouse curiosity in the children and stir in them the confidence to explore and find out things for themselves?
3. Are areas of the classroom devoted to different activities where children can play and learn on their own, similar to the learning centers described in this chapter?
4. Does the child care program build language skills by encouraging children to communicate their ideas and feelings with others and to listen to the ideas and feelings of others?
5. Does the teacher ask questions to encourage the children to think further about the ideas they express?
6. Do they encourage children to give their opinions and solve problems?
7. Do teachers regularly write down the stories the children make up, thereby showing children the connection between their ideas and the written word?
8. Do teachers ask the children why, where, and how questions when children tell stories?
9. Are children encouraged to love books by listening to stories and acting them out, thereby connecting the stories to the pictures and the printed words on the pages?

10. Is the atmosphere at the child care center one of relaxed activity, encouraging learning in a warm, supportive setting that gives children the motivation to learn? Or is learning to read and work with numbers done in a way that causes stress among children and discourages them if they don't immediately achieve success? Is the children's work always on display to encourage a sense of pride in the things they do?

11. Does the program encourage the development of socialization skills among children, teaching them things like sharing and taking turns that are important for success in school?

12. Do teachers plan activities and games so that children gain optimum learning experiences from them?

13. Do teachers join in and share the children's interests?

14. Do teachers show the children that they respect their thoughts and ideas by complimenting them for their expressions, efforts, and achievements?

15. Above all, do children enjoy the classroom and the activities in which they are engaged as they are learning new things?

Epilogue

Suddenly, everyone is talking about universal preschool. But talk is easy. Will states commit the money needed to guarantee quality or try to do preschool on the cheap?

—David L. Kirp
All My Children, article in Education Life section
The New York Times, July 31, 2005

We began this book by writing that Rosa Lee Young is a setting that inspires both hope and tragedy. Hope because it shows what great potential there is in a good early child care program and what it can do for children, tragedy because despite the vast need, there are too few places like Rosa Lee Young in our country today.

I was struck by this fact when I found a leaflet on the windshield of my car as I returned to it in a shopping mall parking lot. The leaflet was headed "Stay at Home Mom. Baby Sitting Services." The text read, "Great references, good atmosphere, cleanliness, and expect only the best from your baby caregiver. You will not be disappointed" and it gave a name and phone number. The person advertising this way could be wonderful or she could be horrible. But the idea of parents having to rely on this kind of child care instead of a proven program at a recognized child care center because they are either too expensive or there aren't enough of them is shocking. A child care worker is entrusted with the well-being of your child. In a similar vein, a doctor is entrusted with your health but can anyone imagine patients having to seek a doctor in this way?

Obviously, we have a long way to go before we can boast of a system of early child care that approaches many of the world's other industrialized democracies. Absent a national, publicly funded early child care program, good child care is still expensive. It is, therefore, available largely for people who can afford it, or for poor people whose income is low enough for Head Start or for some scholarship assistance. Low pay continues to haunt the profession, a huge obstacle to getting highly qualified educators to enter and remain in the field.

However, we end this book not on the note of tragedy but of hope. There is an old Chinese proverb: The longest journey begins with a single step. Early child care is now on the minds of many people. It is making its way even into our legislative halls where there have been calls in some states for a more extensive, affordable program for working parents. As we wrote previously in this book, articles have appeared in the press in the last few years referring to new initiatives on child care. In a few rare cases, companies are setting up child care centers for working parents in their employ—an ideal arrangement for parents who can take some time during the day to drop in to see their children and their children's teachers. It's just a start. But perhaps it's that single step of the long journey that will provide high-quality early child care to every American family who needs it and wants it.

We wrote this book because we believe that there are some wonderful things we can learn from the Rosa Lee Young experience, as there is from other high-quality child care centers. They are proving every day that an excellent child care program is possible. To visit a school like this and see the program in action, to spend several hours there and suddenly realize that you rarely hear a child crying, that the children seem so happy, so engrossed in their play tasks, their minds absorbing the world around them like sponges sopping up water, is to recognize the kind of school experience they are getting right from the beginning.

Child care centers like Rosa Lee Young are providing the first steps in that journey for which all of us must be grateful.

Appendix A

Rosa Lee Young Curriculum Outline

PREKINDERGARTEN AND KINDERGARTEN

The typical day is divided into several different blocks of time for activities and learning experiences of the child, as outlined in the charts shown here:

1. Group time: Children meet together as a class for a particular class activity.
2. Work or activity time: Children have an opportunity to choose to work in the interest centers of their choice throughout the day in the morning or afternoon. Teacher-directed activities are offered for the children to participate in during this time.
3. Breakfast, lunch, snack
4. Rest time
5. Outdoor time

ACTIVITIES AND LEARNING EXPERIENCES THROUGHOUT THE DAY

1. Group Time

Literature activities, music and movement activities, class discussions, and teacher demonstrations take place in the morning and afternoon group times as whole-group activities, as well as throughout the day in small groups and with individual children.

Activity Area	Understanding or Skill Acquired by Children
Group Meeting Area/ Library Area *Rosa Lee Young Childhood Center maintains a school library for classroom use and a "lending library" for child/parent use. In addition, all classes visit the Rockville Centre Public Library for story time with the librarians, to choose books to borrow for use in classrooms, and to participate in the various events and activities provided for children at the library.* *Classroom resources include picture dictionaries, creative work on walls and large charts created by children and teachers to document activities and events.* *Books and other printed materials, clipboards, charts, labels, pens, pencils, and paper are generally included in various learning centers of the classroom.*	**Listening to stories/oral reading:** to develop listening skills, become familiar with story elements and a variety of genres; alphabet books, poems, informational text, fiction, nonfiction; to develop an appreciation of reading and literature; to use literature to learn about new concepts in a variety of disciplines—math, science, social studies; and to begin new projects based upon children's interests **Book discussions:** to learn about authors and illustrators, compare stories, discuss themes and outcomes, and share personal experiences similar to book characters; to ask questions to clarify parts of the text **Retell stories:** to use visual cues to follow story line, demonstrate understanding of story plot and sequence, distinguish between print and pictures, track words and sentences as they are read aloud, read familiar words **Story dramatizations:** to recreate the sequence of a story, demonstrate understanding of character and plot, work as a team to dramatize the story **Music and movement:** to sing and respond to songs and fingerplays; chant and respond to rhymes and poems; make and use simple rhythm instruments; create, respond, and move to rhythmic sounds; respond to recorded and live performances

2. Work or Activity Time

Children have an opportunity to choose to work in the various interest centers of their choice throughout the day. Teacher-directed activities are offered for the children to participate in at work time during the day.

Children also visit places in the community to help develop the child's understanding of the community and how it works. Children visit the fire department, library, pet stores, florist, nurseries, and other places to extend their knowledge and build on the classroom activities.

Activity Area	Understanding or Skill Acquired by Children
Creative Arts Center	Children use a variety of media (paint, markers, crayons, stamps, scissors, staplers, tape, pencils, pens, finger paints, glue, paste, playdough) for personal expression. Creative art activities support all curriculum areas, for example, drawing a picture of a math activity such as an addition problem, representing a science experiment of sinking and floating, or mixing primary colors to get secondary colors. Children build visual and spatial relationship skills to support the emergent writing and develop fine motor/small muscle skills and tactile senses to strengthen eye-hand coordination. Children use imagination to create and respond to a variety of experiences, and they learn to manipulate objects in a meaningful way.

Activity Area	Understanding or Skill Acquired by Children
Writing Center	Children will create a drawing to represent a letter or word or to tell a story, copy or trace letters of the alphabet and practice emergent writing skills. Children and teachers will create class books that are fashioned in the style of a particular author.
Dramatic Play Area	Language and literacy skills are developed and strengthened as children engage in role play such as grocery shopping, taking telephone messages, and mailing letters. They learn to speak more precisely to communicate their own experiences and emotions.
Math/Manipulative Area	Children have an opportunity to manipulate a wide variety of materials in order to develop math skills and understandings. The math area is well stocked with many sets of objects of all sizes, shapes, and colors. Children use materials to develop the following skills and understandings: • Math reasoning: similarities and differences, sorting and classifying, number sequence, quantity, grouping, sequencing • Numbers and numeration: one-to-one correspondence, order of whole numbers, whole and parts, recognizing numbers from 0 to 9 • Modeling and representation: using manipulatives to understand spatial relationships, ordering sets of objects, identifying objects with geometric shapes • Measurement: using standard and nonstandard units of measure; using comparative terms such as more-less, heavier-lighter; comparing length, height, weight, and capacity; gathering and displaying information about objects • Patterns: identifying patterns in the indoor and outdoor equipment; using manipulatives such as puzzles, blocks, and beads to recreate patterns in the environment and to create original patterns; drawing or describing patterns • Motor skills: developing small muscle/fine motor skills to strengthen eye-hand coordination • Language skills: using precise descriptive words, sharing ideas and information, asking questions, making predictions
Block Area	Block play supports all areas of development: • Social skills development: Children interact and negotiate as they share materials, space, and ideas. They alternate between leadership and supportive roles while creating complex structures. They learn to take into account the point of view of others in order to successfully complete projects. • Cognitive skills development: – Math learning takes place as children explore space, size, shape, numbers, part or whole, inside and outside space, measurement. – Science understandings include concepts such as balance and force.

(Continued)

Activity Area	Understanding or Skill Acquired by Children
Block Area (Continued)	– Language skills are enhanced as children use precise names of blocks, discuss plans, role play with the structures created, and explain design to adults and classmates. – Reading and writing skills are developed as children and adults make signs to label structures, dictate stories about structures to teachers for them to write and post in classrooms, draw pictures of their structures, and write words to name and describe them. – Social science understandings are developed as children pretend and act out roles that adults play in society while constructing their projects. They make connections to the world of work, language, and culture, and develop an understanding of their place and value in the family and community at large. – Gross motor skills are strengthened as children lift and haul some of the larger heavier blocks for their projects.

Science Area	Children manipulate and explore a variety of materials and objects as they develop concepts about the world we live in. Key concepts fall into two categories: (1) the physical setting and (2) the living environment.
	
	1. As they explore the physical setting, children have an opportunity to observe and describe properties of objects both indoors and outdoors. They classify objects based on specific criteria and use simple tools to gather and describe information about objects. They combine ingredients to form new substances. Change and the conditions in the environment that cause change are observed. Children are asked to make and record predictions. Observations are made that support or disprove the predictions.
	    Some of the materials used are magnifying glasses, magnets, sorting trays, containers of different sizes, eye droppers, tubes, simple machines such as incline planes and wheels, balls, straws, water, and absorbent paper.
	    Seasonal and weather changes provide for a wide variety of activities such as predicting what will happen to snow when it is brought indoors and discovering the effect water and rain have on the playground.
	
	2. Activities that support learning about the living environment include identifying similarities and differences between living and nonliving things; describing and comparing human and animal habitats; naming parts of human and animal bodies and their functions; naming parts of flowers and plants; identifying ways plants are used for food; and observing, describing, and documenting the growth of living things.
	    There is a variety of class pets to be cared for and observed at Rosa Lee Young: hamsters, guinea pigs, fish, and frogs. In the spring the children create a caterpillar farm and predict and observe the metamorphosis to butterflies. Tadpoles are brought in and observed as they change to frogs. Trips to the local pet shop offer

Activity Area	Understanding or Skill Acquired by Children
Science Area	the children an opportunity to observe and learn about the many exotic fish, birds, and mammals. Children discuss their own growth and compare their physical characteristics as babies to their current characteristics. Gardening is an important part of the learning process. Plants are cared for during the year. They are grown from seed and given as gifts. An outdoor garden in spring and summer includes flowers and vegetables. Food and its origins are explored. Children participate in cooking activities. Nutrition education and proper personal care is explored. Field trips to local nurseries, dentists, and other places are included.
Water and Sand Table Area	Water and sand are open-ended materials that provide opportunities to explore science, math, and language, as children discover their properties, experiment with capacity and volume, learn new vocabulary, create play marine environments, or recreate the world of dinosaurs. Predictions and observation of objects sinking and floating are common. Adding substances such as food coloring or soap to water provides new discoveries. Mixing water in sand allows for new sensory experiences and creative exploration of the resulting mixture. Changing the accessory materials used with water or sand provides for new learning. These materials include water wheels, clear tubes, hand pumps, and rocks.
Computer Area	Computers are found in pre-K, kindergarten, and school-age classrooms. Programs are appropriate for the ages of children in each class. Children develop computer skills as they manipulate the mouse and choose programs. Social skills are strengthened as children wait for turns and work together to complete tasks. Language, reading, and math skills are strengthened as children use content-specific programs. Children also develop vocabulary and language skills as they use language to explain what they are doing and how they are manipulating programs.

3. **Breakfast, Lunch, Snack Time**

    These social times allow children to relax with classmates and teachers and to share personal stories, to discuss the events of the day, and to make future plans. Meals are served family style.

    All meals are prepared according to the Child and Adult Food Care Program guidelines and are nutritious and balanced. Children have an opportunity to discuss healthy eating habits and likes and dislikes, and to explore textures, flavors, and temperatures of foods.

    Children practice personal hygiene as they wash their hands before meals. They help set the tables and clean up afterward.

4. **Rest Time**

    Rest time is a requirement set forth in the Office of Children and Family Services regulations. Teachers use this time to introduce a variety of music—classical, children's—or to play story tapes for children to listen to as they relax and fall asleep.

Quiet activities are available for children as they awaken or for those who do not sleep (drawing and writing materials, books, puzzles, and so on).

5. Outdoor Time (a.m. and p.m.)
Children have the greatest opportunities to develop gross motor skills while engaging in outdoor activities. Equipment and materials are provided for them to climb, run, catch and throw, pedal, push, dig, and carry.

Older children have an opportunity to participate in games with rules and team sports. Younger children play simple games with teachers and classmates.

TODDLER ACTIVITIES AND LEARNING EXPERIENCES THROUGHOUT THE DAY

1. Mealtimes (Breakfast, Lunch, Snack)

Activity/Learning Experience	Understanding and Skill Development
Washing hands	Fine motor, care of personal needs, health
Pouring cereal, milk	Eye-hand coordination, cause and effect of mixing food
Opening cereal container	Fine motor
Getting a chair	Gross motor
Picking a chair	Choice, concept development (color)
Engaging in conversation ("What did you do yesterday? What will you do this morning?"); review and preview	Asking and responding to questions, language development, language extension, vocabulary development, understanding time (before/after)
Request items ("More milk")	Language and development, decisions and discussions, care of needs
Passing napkins	Fine motor, social development
Peeling fruit	Fine motor, health and nutrition
Tasting a variety of foods (apple, orange, banana)	Discrimination, discovery of differences, making comparisons, taste, language development (sour, sweet, soft, hard, cold)
Cutting banana	Fine motor
Using utensils	Fine motor, eye-hand coordination
Passing out dishes, utensils, and portions	One-to-one communication, math (more, less, one, two)
Clean up	Gross motor, fine motor, care of needs, building community

2. Water Table

Activity/Learning Experience	Understanding and Skill Development
Filling water table	Science (hot/cold)
Filling container	Eye-hand coordination, math concepts (full/empty, heavy/light, big/little, more/less), comparing weight
Getting smock from hook	Care of needs, cause and effect, responsibility
Putting on smock	Gross motor, independence, competence
Putting caps on bottles	Fine motor, one-to-one communication, size discrimination, comparing sizes
Filling squeeze bottles	Eye-hand coordination, concept of full/empty
Squeeze bottles	Fine motor, gross motor, cause and effect
Sponges	Fine motor, cause and effect, concept of wet/dry
Using materials (corks, rocks)	Science concepts (sinking/floating, heavy/light)
Wiping spills	Cause and effect, care of needs, responsibility to group
Talking with teachers and peers	Language development, vocabulary development, using precise descriptive language, communication, discussing
Hanging up smocks	Gross motor, care of needs, responsibility
Working with peers	Language development, negotiating skills, sharing, social development, working in groups

3. Outdoor Activity (a.m. and p.m.)

Activity/Learning Experience	Understanding and Skill Development
Running	Gross motor development, understanding body in space
Climbing	Gross motor development, understanding body in space
Jumping	Gross motor development
Digging	Gross motor development, eye-hand coordination
Carrying	Gross motor development, understanding weight, comparisons (heavy/light, more/less)
Throwing balls	Gross motor development, eye-hand coordination
Kicking balls	Gross motor development
Filling and dumping	Gross motor development, understanding space, understanding comparison measurements
Observing nature: trees, birds, flowers, seasons, weather (snow, rain)	Science: weather, seasons, ecosystems, biology (birds, plants)
Observing community workers (garbage collectors, gardeners, food delivery, police and fire vehicles)	Social studies: understanding community workers and the jobs they perform
Gathering information (about seasons, world)	Science
Comparing	Understanding concepts of hot/cold, wet/dry, windy/calm and their effects
Appropriate clothing	Understanding what clothing is appropriate for different seasons and weather (boots, raincoats)
Getting dressed (putting on gloves, jackets, bathing suits)	Gross motor development, fine motor development, sequencing (what comes first when we get dressed), care of needs, understanding weather (what we need to wear in winter/summer)
Rolling toys	Gross motor development, using both sides of body in a pattern (pedaling)

4. Other Activities

Activity/Learning Experience	Understanding and Skill Development
Pretending (mommy, daddy, other family members, policemen, firefighters, ball players)	Developing the imagination, taking another point of view, understanding jobs, communicating with others, developing language , using more precise language
Pretend cooking	Developing language, practicing family roles, using precise language, working with others
Games	Understanding rules, working with others, taking another point of view
Legos and finger painting	Constructing, developing imagination, working with others, developing creativity
Telling stories with whole body	Retelling familiar tales in a new setting, language development, creativity, using more precise language

5. Greeting/Separating

Activity/Learning Experience	Understanding and Skill Development
Hanging up jacket	Gross motor development, fine motor development, care of needs, understanding where things belong, responsibility, recognition of symbol on cubby and hook (prereading)
Saying goodbye to parents	Separating, autonomy, social/emotional, competence Emotional development: – I am competent. – I can survive without my parent with me at all times. Trust parent will return: – Teacher will care for me. – The world is a safe and interesting place. Language development (using more precise language)
Entering classroom	Social/emotional development: – People know who I am. – I can be myself. – My style is respected. – I am a unique person.
Greeting peers	Prosocial development, language development
Teacher communication with parents	As parents drop children off, they share information about individual children (events of previous day or evening). This helps to understand families and their cultures. In addition, teachers share observations about children's days.

6. Group Time

The toddlers gather as an entire class only at meals. Group time is a time when small groups of children gather spontaneously in self-directed activities or with teachers in teacher-initiated activities. These group times take place during morning and afternoon work time as well as early morning and late afternoon greeting and reunion times when parents drop off or pick up children.

Activity/Learning Experience	Understanding and Skill Development
Reading books to children, independent reading	Learning that books contain stories, that they are read from front to back, that literature is enjoyable and informative; learning that letters stand for sounds and words and that pictures relate to the words; phonetic awareness; small motor development (turning pages); large motor development (carrying books); books are informative, interesting, and enjoyable; learning to choose books

Appendix B

Developmentally Appropriate Practice in Early Childhood Programs Serving Children From Birth Through Age 8

—Excerpted and adapted from position paper of the
National Association for the Education of Young Children

This position paper was designed to be used in conjunction with NAEYC's *Criteria for High Quality Early Childhood Programs* (1991) and with *Guidelines for Appropriate Curriculum Content and Assessment in Programs Serving Children Ages 3 through 8* (1992, 1995). It was drawn up with an eye toward the enormous changes that were taking place in daily life and work at the turn of the twenty-first century and the need to prepare children to live as adults in such a rapidly changing world.

Examples of these principles of developmentally appropriate practice are illustrated throughout the text of this book. Where the discussion in the text is particularly illustrative of one of the principles outlined here, the author has included in brackets and boldface type the chapter and pages in the text in which the item is discussed. If no pages are included, the entire chapter is devoted to dealing with the question.

I. When today's children become adults, they will need to

1. Communicate well, respect others, work out differences of opinion and function well in working as a team
2. Analyze situations, make reasoned judgments, and solve problems as they come along
3. Access information through spoken and written language and understand and use new technologies as they are developed
4. Continue to learn new approaches, skills, and knowledge as conditions and needs change

5. Acquire basic academic skills—literacy, mathematical, science, social studies (including history and geography), music and the visual arts, physical education and health [**Chapter 4, page 77; Chapter 6, pages 115–119; Appendix A, pages 134–137**]

6. Develop a positive self-identity and a tolerance for others whose perspective and experience may be different from theirs [**Chapter 3, pages 58–60, 68–71; Chapter 5, pages 86–88, 90–93, 95–97**]

II. Principles of child development and learning that give rise to developmentally appropriate practices

1. Areas of development—physical, social, emotional, cognitive—are closely related. Development in one area influences and are influenced by development in other areas [**Chapter 6**].

2. This development occurs in a relatively orderly sequence, with skills building upon previously acquired skills [**Chapter 4; Appendix A**].

3. Development proceeds at varying rates from child to child as well as unevenly within different areas of each child's functioning. Given the enormous variation among children of the same chronological age, a child's age must be recognized as only a crude index of developmental maturity [**Chapter 1, pages 6–9; Chapter 2, pages 42–44**].

4. Early experiences have both cumulative and delayed effects on individual children's development; optimal periods exist for certain types of development and learning. These early experiences, either positive or negative, are cumulative in the sense that if an experience occurs occasionally, it may have minimal effects. If positive or negative experiences occur frequently, however, they can have lasting, even "snowballing" effects. There is a growing body of research demonstrating that social and sensory motor experiences during the first three years directly affect the neurological development of the brain with important and lasting implications for children's capacity to learn [**Chapter 2**].

5. Development proceeds in predictable directions toward greater complexity, organization, and internalization. Developmentally appropriate programs provide opportunities for children to learn by providing a variety of firsthand experiences and by helping children acquire symbolic knowledge through representing their experiences in a variety of media such as drawing, painting, construction, dramatic play, and written and verbal descriptions [**Chapter 3; Appendix A, pages 134–137; Appendix C**].

6. Development and learning occur in and are influenced by multiple social and cultural contexts. Children's development is best understood within the sociocultural context of the family, educational setting, community, and broader society [**Chapter 2, pages 48–54; Chapter 5, pages 89–94**].

7. Children are active learners, drawing on direct physical and social experience as well as culturally transmitted knowledge to construct their own understandings of the world around them [**Chapter 5, pages 99–100; Chapter 6, pages 106–110, 114–117**].

8. Development and learning result from interaction of biological maturation and the environment, which includes both the physical and social worlds that children live in [**Chapter 3, pages 60–69**].

9. Play is an important vehicle for children's social, emotional, and cognitive development as well as a reflection of their development [**Chapter 6, pages 110–117**].

10. Development advances when children have opportunities to practice newly acquired skills as well as when they experience a challenge just beyond the level of their present mastery [**Chapter 3**].

11. Children demonstrate different modes of knowing and learning and different ways of representing what they know [**Chapter 6; Appendix C**].

12. Children develop and learn best in the context of a community where they are safe and valued, their physical needs are met, and they feel psychologically secure [**Chapter 2**]. Because children's physical health and safety too often are threatened today, programs for young children must provide not only adequate health, safety, and nutrition but also more comprehensive services such as physical, dental, and mental health and social services [**Chapter 1, pages 22–23**]. In addition, children's development in all areas is influenced by their ability to maintain a limited number of positive, consistent primary relationships with adults and with other children [**Chapters 2 and 3**]. These primary relationships begin in the family but extend over time to include children's teachers and members of the community; therefore, practices that are developmentally appropriate address children's physical, social, and emotional needs as well as their intellectual development [**Chapter 6**].

III. Guidelines for decisions about developmentally appropriate practice

(Early childhood professionals draw on all these fundamental ideas, as well as many others, when making decisions about their practice.)

1. Creating a caring community of learners: Developmentally appropriate practices occur within a context that supports the development of relationships between adults and children, among children, among teachers, and between teachers and families [**Chapter 2; Chapter 3; Chapter 6**].

A. Social relationships are an important context for learning. Each child has strengths or interests that contribute to the overall functioning of the group. When children have opportunities to play together, work on projects in small groups, and talk with other children and adults, their own development and learning are enhanced [**Chapter 3**].

B. The learning environment is supportive of children's physiological needs for activity, sensory stimulation, fresh air, rest, and nourishment. The program provides a balance of rest and active movement for children throughout the program day. Outdoor experiences are provided for children of all ages. The program also protects children's psychological safety; that is, children feel secure, relaxed, and comfortable rather than disengaged, frightened, worried, or stressed [**Appendix A**].

C. The learning environment provides a variety of materials and opportunities for children to have firsthand, meaningful experiences.

2. Teaching to enhance development and learning: Adults are responsible for ensuring children's healthy development and learning. From birth, relationships with adults are critical determinants of children's healthy social and emotional development and serve as well as mediators of language and intellectual development. At the same time, children are active constructors of their own understanding, who benefit from initiating and regulating their own learning activities and interacting with peers. Therefore, early childhood teachers strive to achieve optimal balance between children's self-initiated learning and adult guidance or support. Teachers use their knowledge of child development and learning to identify the range of activities, materials, and learning experiences that are appropriate for a group or individual child. The following guidelines are among those that describe aspects of the teachers' role in making decisions about practice [**Chapter 2, pages 36–38, 42–46**]:

A. Teachers respect, value, and accept children and treat them with dignity at all times.

B. Teachers make it a priority to know each child well.

   • Teachers are alert to signs of undue stress and traumatic events in the children's lives and aware of effective strategies to reduce stress and support the development of resilience [**Chapter 2**].

   • Teachers plan for children's increasing development and self-regulation abilities [**Chapter 1, pages 6–9; Chapter 4, pages 76–77**].

C. Teachers create an intellectually engaging, responsive environment to promote each child's learning and development [**Chapter 4; Chapter 6**].

   • Teachers offer children the choice to participate in a small-group or a solitary activity, assist and guide children who are not yet able to use and enjoy child-choice activity periods, and provide opportunities for practice of skills as a self-chosen activity.

   • Teachers organize the daily and weekly schedule and allocate time to provide children with extended blocks of time in which to engage in play or projects, or study in integrated curriculum [**Chapter 4, page 77; Chapter 6, pages 117–119; Appendix A**].

D. Teachers make plans to enable children to attain key curriculum goals across various disciplines such as language arts, mathematics, social studies, science, art, music, and physical education and health **[Chapter 4, page 77; Chapter 6, pages 117–119; Appendix A, pages 134–137, 138–141]**.

E. Teachers foster children's collaboration with peers on interesting, important enterprises **[Chapter 3]**.

- Teachers use a variety of ways of flexibly grouping children for instruction, supporting collaboration among children, and building a sense of community. At various times children have opportunities to work individually, in small groups, and with the whole group.

F. Teachers develop, refine, and use a wide repertoire of teaching strategies to enhance children's learning and development. These strategies include but are not limited to **[Chapter 4, pages 75–76; Chapter 6, pages 108–110, 114–122; Appendix A, pages 134–137]**:

- Encouraging children to choose and plan their activities

- Posing questions and problems that stimulate creative thinking.

- Using teaching strategies like verbal encouragement, reinforcement, and other behavioral procedures

- Modifying equipment and previously planned schedules as needed

- Guiding children directly in specific skills, including one-on-one attention where necessary while another teacher engages the rest of the class

- Adapting the complexity of the tasks to suit children's level of skill and knowledge and using cues and other forms of scaffolding to enable the child to succeed in a task that may be just beyond his ability to complete alone **[Chapter 1, pages 11–17; Chapter 4, page 77; Appendix A]**.

- Encouraging children to reflect on and revisit their learning experiences **[Chapter 6, pages 108–110, 116–117]**.

G. Teachers facilitate the development of responsibility and self-regulation in children. This includes the following **[Chapter 1, pages 6–9; Chapter 2, pages 42–46; Chapter 3, pages 69–71; Chapter 5, pages 95–97]**:

- Setting clear, consistent, and fair limits on children's behavior

- Redirecting children to more acceptable behavior or activity, using their mistakes as learning opportunities by reminding them of rules and their rationale as needed

- Listening to children and acknowledging their feelings and frustrations, and responding with respect as they guide children to resolve conflicts, exhibiting the skills children need to solve their own problems **[Chapter 2, pages 38–40; Chapter 3, pages 69–71]**

3. Constructing a developmentally appropriate curriculum that provides for all areas of a child's development—physical, emotional, social, linguistic, aesthetic, and cognitive—and stimulates them to go on learning **[Chapter 4, pages 75–77; Appendix A]**

  A. The curriculum includes a broad range of content across disciplines that is socially relevant, intellectually engaging, and personally meaningful to children.

  B. It builds upon what children already know to foster the acquisition of new concepts and skills.

  C. It provides opportunities to support children's home culture and language while also developing children's abilities to participate in the shared culture of the community **[Chapter 5, pages 87–88, 90–94]**.

  D. It makes use of technology that is physically and philosophically integrated into the classroom curriculum and teaching.

4. Assessing children's learning and development: In a developmentally appropriate curriculum, assessment and curriculum are integrated with teachers continually engaging in observational assessment for improving teaching and learning **[Chapter 4]**.

  A. The content of assessments reflects progress toward important learning and developmental goals.

  B. The methods of assessment are appropriate to the age and experiences of young children **[Chapter 1, pages 9–12; Appendix A]**.

  C. Decisions that have a major impact on children, such as enrollment and placement, are never made on the basis of a single developmental assessment or screening device but are based on multiple sources of relevant information, particularly observations by teachers and parents.

5. Establishing reciprocal relationships with families in which mutual respect, cooperation, and shared responsibility are the key ingredients **[Chapter 2, pages 48–53]**. This means that

  A. The program and the teachers work in collaborative partnership with families with regular, frequent, two-way communication between them. They share their knowledge of the child as part of day-to-day communication and planned conferences.

  B. Parents are welcomed into the program and participate in discussions about their child's care and education.

  C. Teachers acknowledge and are respectful about parents' choices and goals for their children. They respond with sensitivity to parents' preferences and concerns without abdicating their professional responsibility to children.

  D. The program links families with a range of services based on identified resources, priorities, and concerns.

IV. There is a strong interrelationship between child development and learning—it is not an either/or situation [**Chapter 6**].

    1. Children benefit from being challenged to practice newly acquired skills and from the opportunities to gain the confidence in themselves to persist at a task until they meet with success.

    2. They benefit from predictable structure and orderly routine in the learning environment and from the teacher's flexibility and spontaneity in responding to their emerging ideas, needs, and interests [**Chapter 1, pages 9–11; Chapter 2, pages 40–41**].

    3. They benefit from instruction by more competent peers and adults [**Chapter 2, pages 42–46; Chapter 3, pages 58–59; Chapter 6, pages 108–110**].

    4. At the same time, they benefit from opportunities to collaborate with their peers to acquire a sense of being part of a community and from being treated as individuals in their own strengths, interests, and needs [**Chapter 2, pages 42–44; Chapter 3, pages 58–60**].

    5. Children need to develop a positive sense of their own self-identity and respect for other people whose perspectives and experiences may be different from their own [**Chapter 5, pages 89–94**].

V. Policies essential to achieving developmentally appropriate practice in early childhood programs: Early childhood professionals working in diverse situations with varying levels of funding and resources are responsible for implementing practices that are developmentally appropriate for the children they serve. However, the kinds of practices necessary for high-quality child care are more likely to be implemented within an infrastructure of supportive policies and resources. Policymaking groups at the state and local levels should consider the following when implementing early childhood programs:

    1. A comprehensive professional preparation and development system is in place to ensure that early childhood programs are staffed with qualified personnel: This system includes higher education, ongoing inservice training, well-qualified and supportive administrators, and available specialists for children with individual special needs [**Introduction, Chapter 1, pages 23–27; Chapter 4, pages 78–81**].

    2. Adequate funding for staffing, including professional-level compensation for qualified personnel to ensure the effective recruitment and retention of highly skilled, trained, and competent staff and to guarantee appropriate teacher-child ratios for each age group [**Introduction; Box: The Physical Set-Up of a Child Care Center, page 21**].

    3. Adequate resources and materials for safe, stimulating learning environments.

4. Adequate systems for regulating and monitoring the quality of early childhood programs
5. Availability of community resources for special needs of children and their families **[Chapter 1, pages 22–23]**.

Appendix C

Reggio Emilia

REGGIO EMILIA AND THE
HUNDRED LANGUAGES OF CHILDREN

In her twenty-five years as director of the Rosa Lee Young Childhood Center, Joan Sheppard attended a lot of conferences on infant, toddler, and preschool care. Conferences on philosophy. Conferences on methodology. On child psychology. Plenty of speakers. Lots of seminars. Loads of discussion. But none affected her thinking and her approach to children as much as the one in the early nineties in which she heard a group of Italian visitors to our country.

They were from a small city very few people had ever heard of, Reggio Emilia (population 130,000) in the Po River valley of northern Italy, and they were here on a professional tour of the United States to talk about the system of infant-toddler centers and preschools in their home town. Created by some local communities in the aftermath of World War II—the first schools of any kind in the war's aftermath in Reggio Emilia were built by parents with their own hands and financed from the sale of an old tank and some army trucks and horses—the city administration in 1971 made the preschools and infant-toddler centers part of its public educational system. It now devotes about 14 percent of its municipal budget to the network of twenty preschools and thirteen infant-toddler centers that serve more than three thousand, or close to 95 percent, of the city's preschoolers, and nearly a thousand, or about 35 percent, of its infants and toddlers.

Sheppard, now retired, met the group of preschool educators from Reggio Emilia at one of the workshops on its visit to the United States in 1993 and was deeply impressed by what she heard, particularly from the founder of the Reggio schools, the late Loris Malaguzzi. "He could inspire anybody," she recalled. She became friendly and began a professional dialogue with the group, exchanging ideas and notes about their craft. Several years later, she was part of a study group of American early childhood educators who visited the Italian city, observed its schools, and spoke with its teachers and administrators. What she came away with was a picture that provided a keen insight into what a deeply committed program of early child care can do for children.

"Reggio is fascinating in the dedication these people have to young children" and although "you can't make a Reggio school here—it's a whole world apart—you can certainly take their philosophy and apply it here," Sheppard said. "Certainly we can apply their philosophy of the image of the child. They look at a child and look at his strengths. While they recognize the deficits and know what has to be done, they don't focus on the deficits and forget about that child. They feel that every child has something to bring and that children need to use all the languages available to them."

That philosophy was the cornerstone of her work as director of the Rosa Lee Young Childhood Center.

The Reggio outlook on early child care attracted great attention with an exhibit of the work of its children that toured Europe for many years and came to North America more than twenty years ago. The exhibit was called *The Hundred Languages of Children* and was based upon the fact that children need to express themselves in many forms: dance, music, art, performance, as well as learning to read and write.

"We believe that the brain is not imprisoned by the genes," wrote Malaguzzi in the catalogue of *The Hundred Languages of Children* exhibit, "that thought can be modified inasmuch as it interacts with the environment, and that intelligence is the result of the synergistic cooperation of the various parts of the brain. For this reason, we maintain that children are born with all the languages of life. These languages are intricate by nature. . . . The more languages we recognize in children, the more we can help them act and identify the *methodological models* they need for confronting events and experiences . . . in a constructive process that is applicable to all learning."

Malaguzzi believed that each school should create its own environment rather than having one fostered upon it as a norm and that the environment "should act as a kind of aquarium" that reflects the attitudes and culture of the children in it.

He was also a strong advocate of parent and community participation in the educational process of young children. The Reggio Emilia philosophy is that there is a kind of social pact between the parents and the school based not merely on courtesy but on the real practice of relationships and communication through dialogue and exchange. In addition, it is essential that the infant-toddler center and preschool be open and welcoming places for everyone, children and parents alike.

Children's progress is documented through transcriptions of children's remarks, photographs of their activities, and multimedia representations of their thinking. Parents don't come to see just the finished product, Sheppard said, but to get an explanation of how it came to be so they can see how their children are speaking in the many languages they use.

And often the explanation is more fascinating than the finished product itself. Sheppard recounted the story of a child who drew a picture of his house. "He had his bedroom and his living room and his Christmas tree and everything. And then he took the paper and made it all brown so that it was just a brown piece of paper. That was because it was dark at night. But if you only looked at a brown piece of paper, you'd think, 'What the heck are they hanging that up for?' But actually, this was a masterpiece of his expression."

(See *The Municipal Infant-Toddler Centers and Preschools of Reggio Emilia*, Municipality of Reggio Emilia, 1996, pp. 13–17, 19.)

THE NINE BASIC PRINCIPLES OF REGGIO EMILIA

Over the years, the philosophy of the Reggio Emilia infant-toddler centers and preschools has evolved into certain basic principles in the program's day-to-day operation. These principles have become a foundation for good early childhood education anywhere, and, as I observed them, are at the heart of the classroom operations in Rosa Lee Young. Not that they can always be achieved everywhere. Every school has its problems and limitations placed on it by local conditions, and Rosa Lee Young is no exception. But if the basic principles are kept in mind, we're on the way to some measure of success. Summarized, these basic principles are as follows:

1. The image of the child is one in which all children have potential, curiosity, and interest in everything the environment brings to them.
2. Children have rights that should be recognized, and that among them are the right to high-quality care and education, the best that society has to offer, and that these rights are directly associated with the well-being of parents and teachers.
3. Parent participation in the education of their children is essential, and this takes many forms: day-to-day interaction in the schools, discussion of educational and psychological issues, and special events. Parent participation is geared to the principle that parents not only participate in their own child's education but also help ensure the welfare of all children in the school.
4. The school must be a pleasant and joyful place, expressed through the physical layout and through the leisurely and friendly pace of activities. The clock must never be a tyrant, and children must be allowed to proceed with their activities at their own pace.
5. The teacher and the child are partners in learning, with the teacher acting as a resource for the child, asking questions, drawing out the child's ideas and theories, and helping him to discover and learn in the process.
6. Cooperation is the hallmark of the system. Teachers work in pairs as partners, not as head teacher and assistant. All teachers engage in continuous interchange with colleagues, interpreting and upgrading their work, so that their training is ongoing and perpetual. Teachers are assisted by teams of pedagogical coordinators who support their relationships with parents and with community and city administrators.
7. The curriculum evolves from the children's activities and is not set down in advance. Teachers express the general goals and hypotheses about what direction the children's activities and projects may take and

make appropriate preparations, but the curriculum is highly flexible and emerges from the children's activities and projects.

8. Every school has a teacher trained in the visual arts who works closely with the other teachers. A special space, workshop, or studio, called an *atelier*, is set aside in each school for the use of all children and teachers to express themselves through art forms. (At Rosa Lee Young, there is no special art teacher or a separate art studio. In each room is an art area where the regular teacher works with the children as they express themselves through art forms.)

9. The progress of all children is documented through various media that show the thinking process of each project they engage in, through the many languages they use, not just the finished product.

Notes

FOREWORD

1. *Start early, finish strong: How to help every child become a reader*, July 1999.
2. U.S. Department of Education, OERI, 1996.
3. J. B. Shonkoff & D. A. Phillips, *From neurons to neighborhoods*. Harvard Center for the Developing Child, http://www.developingchild.harvard.edu/, 2006.
4. J. Heckman, *Fostering human capital*. Ounce of Prevention Fund, http://www .ounceofprevention.org
5. New Freedom Commission on Mental Health. *Achieving the promise: Transforming mental health care in America.* Final report (DHHS Pub. No. SMA-03-3832), U.S. Department of Health and Human Services, Substance Abuse and Mental Health Services Administration, Rockville, MD, 2003.
6. J. Knitzer & J. Lefkowitz, *Helping the most vulnerable infants, toddlers, and their families* (Pathways to Early School Success Issue Brief No. 1), National Center for Children in Poverty, Columbia University Mailman School of Public Health, New York, NY, 2006.
7. The current federal poverty level for a family of four is $20,000. Low-income families make up to twice that amount. For more information on measuring poverty, see National Center for Children in Poverty's state profiles and the U.S. Department of Health and Human Services.
8. J. Knitzer, *Testimony on the economic and societal costs of poverty*, National Center for Children in Poverty (NCCP), http://www.nccp.org/publications/pub_705.html, 2007
9. W. S. Gilliam, *Prekindergartens left behind: Expulsion rates in state prekindergarten programs* (FCD Policy Brief Series 3), Foundation for Child Development, New York, NY, 2005.
10. *Start early, finish strong: How to help every child become a reader*, http://www.ed.gov/pubs/startearly/ch_2.html, July 1999.
11. J. L. Kreader, D. Ferguson, & S. Lawrence, book description of *Infant and toddler child care quality*, National Center for Children in Poverty, 2005.
12. J. R. Lally, videotape titled *In our hands*, produced by WestEd, San Francisco, CA, 1997.
13. Sameroff & Seifer et al., 1987; Sameroff & Seifer et al., 1993.
14. Commission for Economic Opportunity, 2006.
15. E. Roosevelt, Chairwoman, Commission of Human Rights, in *Universal declaration of human rights*, December 9, 1948.
16. R. Shahmoon Shanok, D. Henderson, D. B. Grellong, & G. Foley, Preparation for practice in an integrated model, in *Mental health in early intervention*, G. Foley, & J. Hochman, (Eds.), 2006, pp. 384, 387.

INTRODUCTION

17. Statistical Abstract of the United States: 2003, U.S. Department of Commerce, Economics and Statistics Administration, U.S. Census Bureau, Charts 597, 598, p. 391.
18. J. R. Lally, *The impact of child care policies and practices on infant/toddler identity formation*, National Association for the Education of Young Children, Vol. 51, No. 1, Nov. 1995, p. 58.
19. J. B. Shonkoff & D. A. Phillips, (Eds.), *From neurons to neighborhoods: The science of early childhood development*, Committee on Integrating the Science of Early Childhood Development, Board on Children, Youth, and Families, National Research Council and Institute of Medicine, National Academy Press, 2000, pp. 297-299.
20. Statistical Abstract of the United States: 2003, op. cit., Chart 598, p. 391.
21. *From neurons to neighborhoods*, op. cit., p. 297.
22. G. Foley, paper presented at 15th National Training Institute of Zero to Three, Nov. 30–Dec. 3, 2000.
23. S. Albin, Taking care of small people is becoming big business, article in Long Island section, *The New York Times*, July 31, 2005.
24. S.W. Helburn, *Cost, quality, and child outcomes in child care centers, technical report*, Department of Economics, Center for Research in Economic and Social Policy, University of Colorado at Denver, 1995, as cited by G. Foley, op. cit.
25. S. Albin, op. cit.

CHAPTER 1

26. G. Foley, paper presented at 15th National Training Institute of Zero to Three, Nov. 30–Dec. 3, 2000.
27. L. Koplow, *Unsmiling faces: How preschools can heal*, Teachers College Press, Columbia University, 1996, p. 3.
28. The Montessori Method, http://www.michaelolaf.net
29. J. R. Lally, et al., (Eds.), *Caring for infants and toddlers in groups: Developmentally appropriate practice*, Zero to Three, 1995, pp. 5–6.
30. N. Becker, *A comprehensive guide for caregivers in day-care settings*, Charles C. Thomas, Ltd., 1999, pp. 19–20.
31. Lally, *Caring for infants and toddlers in groups*, op. cit., p. 7.
32. Shonkoff & Phillips, *From neurons to neighborhoods*, op. cit., pp. 299–300.
33. Lally, *Caring for infants and toddlers in groups*, op. cit., p. 5.
34. A. F. Lieberman, *The emotional life of the toddler*, The Free Press, 1993, pp. 206, 221.
35. S. I. Greenspan, MD, *Building healthy minds: The six experiences that create intelligence and emotional growth in babies and young children*, Perseus Books, 1999, pp. 4, 9.
36. M. A. Graham, A. E. Hogan, B. A. White, & C. A. Chiricos, Enhancing the quality of relationships in infant-toddler child care: A developmental process, *Zero to Three/Journal*, Vol. XXIII, No. 6, July 2003, op. cit., p. 16.
37. K. D. Pruett, MD, *Me, myself and I: How children build their sense of self*, Goddard Press, 1999, p. 50.
38. S. I. Greenspan, MD, *The growth of the mind*, Addison Wesley, 1997, pp. 77, 78, 85.
39. S. I. Greenspan, *Building healthy minds*, op. cit., pp. 227, 327.
40. A. S. Honig & H. E. Brophy, *Talking with your baby: Family as the first school*, Syracuse University Press, 1996, pp. 19–20.
41. S. I. Greenspan, *Great kids: Helping your baby and child develop the 10 essential qualities for a healthy, happy life*, Da Capo Press (Merloyd Lawrence, Perseus Books Group), 2007, p. 39.

42. Graham et al., op. cit., p. 16.
43. T. B. Brazelton, MD, & S. I. Greenspan, MD, *The irreducible needs of children: What every child must have to grow, learn, and flourish*, Perseus Publishing, 2000, p. 79.
44. Graham et al., op. cit., p. 16.
45. Ibid, p. 15.
46. M. Whitebook et al., *Worthy work, unlivable wages: The national child care staffing study, 1988–1997*, Center for Child Care Work Force, 1998, p. 8.

CHAPTER 2

47. R. Shahmoon Shanok, Infant mental health perspectives on peer play: Psychotherapy for symptomatic, at-risk, and disordered young children, Chapter 6, *Handbook of Infant Mental Health*, Volume IV, J. D. Osofsky & H. E. Fitzgerald, (Eds.), World Association for Infant Mental Health, John Wiley & Sons, 2000, p. 204
48. D. J. Siegel, MD, & M. Hartzell, *Parenting from the inside out: How a deeper self-understanding can help you raise children who thrive*, Jeremy P. Tarcher/Putnam, 2003, pp. 101–102.
49. Ibid., pp. 102–103.
50. A. S. Honig, *Secure relationships: Nurturing infant/toddler attachment in early child care settings*, National Association for the Education of Young Children, 2002, pp. 6, 45.
51. R. Parlakian, *Before the ABCs: Promoting school readiness in infants and toddlers*, Zero to Three, 2003, p. 17.
52. *The New York Times*, Week in Review, May 22, 2005.
53. L. Koplow, *Creating schools that heal: Real life solutions*, Teachers College Press, Columbia University, 2002, p. 17.
54. K. C. Gallagher, Brain research and early childhood development: A primer for developmentally appropriate practice, *Young Children: Journal of the National Association for the Education of Young Children*, July 2005, p. 20.
55. S. I. Greenspan, MD, *Building healthy minds*, op. cit, 1999, pp. 267–268.
56. A. Slade, Making meaning and making believe: Their role in the clinical process, in *Children at play: Clinical and developmental approaches to meaning and representation*, A. Slade & D. P. Wolf, (Eds.), Oxford University Press, 1994.
57. A. Honig, *Secure relationships*, op. cit., p. 55, citing A. C. Baker & L.A. Manfredi, *Circle of love: Relationships between parents, providers and children in family child care*, Redleaf, 1998.
58. Ibid., pp. 54–55.
59. M. Olson & M. Hyson, NAEYC explores parental perspectives on early childhood education, *Young Children*, op. cit., May 2005, p. 56–58.
60. A. F. Lieberman, *What is culturally sensitive intervention?*, paper presented at the National Center for Clinical Infant Programs Winter Meetings, Dec. 1987, pp. 10–12.
61. E. Geist & A. C. Baum, Yeah, buts that keep teachers from embracing an active Curriculum: Overcoming the resistance, *Young Children*, op. cit., July 2005, pp. 32–33.

CHAPTER 3

62. *From neurons to neighborhoods*, op. cit., p. 163.
63. L. Koplow, *Unsmiling faces*, op. cit. p. 8.
64. Ibid., p. 24.
65. *From neurons to neighborhoods*, op. cit., p. 166.
66. Ibid., p. 168.

67. J. E. Montie, J. Claxton, & S. D. Lockhart, A multinational study supports child-initiated learning, *Young Children*, op. cit., Nov. 2007, pp. 25–26.

68. S. I. Greenspan, *Great kids*, op. cit., p. 154.

69. J. Brown & K. A. Dodge, Early peer relations and child psychiatry, *Handbook of child and adolescent psychiatry*, Vol. I, John Wiley & Sons, 1997, pp. 305, 306.

70. *From neurons to neighborhoods*, op. cit., pp. 167–168.

71. T. B. Brazelton, MD & S. I. Greenspan, MD, *The irreducible needs of children: What every child must have to grow, learn, and flourish*, Perseus Publishing, 2000, p. 124.

72. D. Trounson-Chaiken, From chaos to cohesion: Group therapy with preschool-aged children, *Journal of Child and Adolescent Group Therapy*, Vol 6, No. 1, 1996.

73. *From neurons to neighborhoods*, op. cit., p. 169.

CHAPTER 4

74. National Association for the Education of Young Children, *Developmentally appropriate practice in early childhood programs serving children from birth through age 8*, (citing the works of Gelman & Baillargeon, A review of some Piagetian concepts, in *Handbook of Child Psychology*, Vol. 3, P. H. Mussey, (Ed.), Wiley, New York, 1983, pp. 167–230; Gelman & Meck, Preschoolers counting: Principles before skill. *Cognition 13*, 1983, pp. 343–359; Edwards, Gandini, & Forman, *The hundred languages of children: The Reggio Emilia approach to early childhood education*, Ablex, Norwood, N.J., 1993; Resnick, Schooling and the workplace: What relationship? in *Preparing youth for the 21st century*, The Aspen Institute, Washington, DC, 1996; and Shepard & Smith, Escalating academic demand in kindergarten: Some nonsolutions, *Elementary School Journal*, Vol. 89, No. 2, pp. 135–146), available at http://www.naeyc.org, Oct. 2007. An abridged version of this NAEYC position paper can be found in Appendix B of this book.

75. *Young Times*, newsletter of the Rosa Lee Young Childhood Center, Oct. 2003.

76. S. L. Kagan, R. N. Brandon, C. H. Ripple, E. J. Maher, & J. M. Joesch, Addressing compensation and infrastructure, *Young Children*, op. cit., May 2002, pp. 58, 60.

77. S. Wolkoff, *Mandated training: Softening the resistance*, Zero to Three, op. cit., June/July 2000, p. 28.

78. T. Norman-Murch & K. Wollenburg, *An integrated approach to supporting professional development through in-service education and supervision*, Zero to Three, op. cit., June/July 2000, p. 18. Internal quotes are from E. Fenichel, *Learning through supervision and mentorship to support the development of infants, toddlers and their families*, Zero to Three, 1992.

79. Ibid., pp. 20–22.

CHAPTER 5

80. As quoted in the *Rockville Centre Herald*, a local weekly newspaper, Nov. 24–30, 2005.

81. Quoted from *Considerations when supporting second language learners*, background supplementary material distributed at panel on Building Language and Literacy in Our Youngest Children at Zero to Three 20th National Training Institute in Washington, DC, Nov. 4, 2005.

82. L. Okagaki & K. E. Diamond, Responding to cultural and linguistic differences in

the beliefs and practices of families with young children, *Young Children*, op. cit., May 2000, p. 77.

83. *Considerations when supporting second language learners*, op. cit.
84. One of Mexico's most important holidays that commemorates the 1862 defeat of French invaders by Mexican forces.
85. B. Kaiser & J. S. Rasminsky, Opening the culture door, *Young Children*, op. cit., July 2003, p. 53.
86. L. Okagaki & K. E. Diamond, op. cit., p. 74.
87. J. Bradley & P. Kibera, Closing the gap: Culture and the promotion of inclusion in child dare, *Young Children*, op. cit., Jan. 2006, p. 34.
88. V. J. Carlson, X. Feng, & R. L. Harwood, *The "ideal baby": A look at the intersection of temperament and culture*, Zero to Three, op. cit., March 2004, p. 22.
89. Ibid., p. 22.
90. B. Kaiser & J. S. Rasminsky, op. cit., pp. 53–54.
91. A. F. Lieberman, *What is culturally sensitive intervention?*, paper presented at the National Center for Clinical Infant Programs Winter Meetings, Dec. 1987, p. 5.
92. Carlson et al., op. cit., p. 24.
93. L. Okagaki & K. E. Diamond, op. cit., pp. 78–79.

CHAPTER 6

94. U. S. Congress, House Committee on Education and Labor, Subcommittee on Postsecondary Education, *Illiteracy and the scope of the problem in this country*, 1984.
95. E. F. Zigler, D. G. Singer, & S. J. Bishop-Josef, *Children's play: The roots of reading*, Zero to Three Press, 2004, p. 3.
96. D. Elkind, *Miseducation: Preschoolers at risk*, Alfred A. Knopf, 1996, pp. 157–158.
97. E. F. Zigler et al., op. cit., p. ix.
98. S. I. Greenspan, *Building healthy minds*, op. cit., pp. 11, 54, 67.
99. D. Breslin, Children's capacity to develop resiliency: How to nurture it, *Young Children*, op. cit., Jan. 2005, p. 47. Also see R. Rosenthal & L. Jacobson, *Pygmalion in the classroom*, Holt, Rinehart & Winston, 1968, p. 3.
100. K. C. Kersey & C. R. Malley, Helping children develop resiliency: Providing supportive relationships, *Young Children*, op. cit., Jan. 2005, p. 53. Also see R. Brooks & S. Goldstein, *Nurturing resilience in our children*, Contemporary Books, 2003, p. 18.
101. Zigler et al., op. cit., pp. 6–7.
102. Ibid., pp. 6–7.
103. R. Shahmoon Shanok, op. cit., p. 206.
104. E. Bodrova & D. J. Leong, Chopsticks and counting chips: Do play and foundational skills need to compete for the teacher's attention in an early childhood classroom?, *Young Children*, op. cit., May 2003, p. 12. Also see K. Roskos & J. Christie, Examining the play literacy interface: A critical review of future directions, *Journal of Early Childhood Literacy*, Vol. I, No. 1, pp. 59–89.
105. Ibid., pp. 13, 16.

Index

Quint, Dr., xxvii
Quint, Mrs., xxv
Quinterno, Barbara, 24, 36–38, 40–41, 63

"Rain sticks," 93
Reading
    adults reading to children, 5, 8, 13, 28, 35, 37,
        47, 110, 117, 120, 124, 134, 142. *See* Stories,
        reading or telling stories to children
    children reading by themselves, 9, 45, 71,
        118, 119, 125, 142
    children's ability to read, 35, 44, 50, 54, 55,
        83, 103, 108, 110, 115, 124, 136, 137, 141.
        See Skills, reading and writing
Reflective thinking, 114
Reggio Emilia, 4, 5, 21, 77, 144, 145, 151–154
    Hundred Languages of Children, 151–153
Relatedness, 113
Relationships
    between children, ix, xii, xxxi, 4, 28, 57–73,
        145. *See* Play
    between parent and child, ix, 5, 9, 11, 28,
        33, 34, 146
    between parent and child care program, 34,
        48–55, 80, 145, 148
    between teacher and child, xi, xxxi, 4,5,
        9–10, 33–48, 106, 145
    between teacher and supervisor, 79–80
Responsibility, teaching of, 44–45, 55, 139, 141,
    147, 148
Rey, Jeannine, 3, 5, 25, 40, 48, 50, 70, 87–90,
    93–97, 107–108, 123
Rickover, Admiral Hyman G. (U.S. Navy),
    104, 105
Robinson, Pepper, 6–13, 14–20, 25, 27, 62, 76,
    106, 118
Rockville Centre (Long Island, New York),
    xix, xx, xxi, xxii, xxiii, xxiv, xxv, 2, 25, 26, 85,
    87, 116, 127, 134
Rockville Centre Herald, 74, 86
Rogers, Fred, 102
Role playing, 24, 38, 59, 62, 80, 83, 114, 118,
    135, 136
Roosevelt, Eleanor, xii
Rosa Lee Young Curriculum, 133–142
    breakfast, lunch, and snack, 133, 137, 138
    group time (listening to stories, retelling
        stories, book discussions, dramatiza-
        tions, music, and movement), 133–134
    learning centers (creative arts, writing,
        dramatic play, math/manipulative,
        blocks, science, water and sand table
        area, computer area). *See* Learning areas
        of room, Learning Centers
    outdoor time, 133, 138

    prekindergarten and kindergarten
        curriculum, 133–138
    rest time, 133, 137
    toddler curriculum, 138–142
    work or activity time, 133, 134–137
Rothschild, Marie, xxiv, xxv
Rules, following, 62, 63, 66, 114, 122, 126, 138,
    141, 147
Rye bread. *See* Breads in different cultures

Safe environment, xi, xxii, xxvi, xxx, 21, 32, 33,
    35, 52, 122, 126, 141, 145, 146, 149. *See*
    Physical set-up of a child care center, health
    and safety of children
Salaries for child care workers, x, xxiii, xxix,
    xxx, 23–25, 27, 78, 79
Sandel, Leonard, xxv
Santa Claus, 96
Scaffolding, 81, 147
Schedules, 18, 40–41, 55, 118–119, 146, 147
Schnitzer, Linda, 1, 25–27, 46–47, 63, 70, 71, 80, 92
School holidays and culture. *See* Holidays
School readiness, xx, 34, 75, 103, 104, 108, 128
Self-confidence, 5, 34, 46, 51, 58, 68, 75, 100,
    106, 112, 113, 128, 149
Self-control, 113. *See* Emotional control
Self-esteem, 11, 30, 59, 66, 73, 75, 106, 107. *See*
    Play, building self-esteem
Self-regulation, 35, 114, 146, 147. *See* Behavior
    self-regulation
Self-reliance. *See* Independence,
    encouragement of
Sensory motor development. *See* Motor
    development
Separation anxiety in children, 9–10, 28, 49,
    76, 84, 127, 141
Sequencing games, 135
Setting limits, 38, 147
Settling disputes between children, 69–71,
    119–120, 122, 123, 125–126
Sexual abuse of children, 43, 46
Shakespeare, 27
Shanok, Rebecca Shahmoon, xii, 32, 112
Sheppard, Joan, xx, xxi, xxii, xxiii, xxiv, xxv,
    xxvi, 26, 77, 87, 92, 127, 151, 152
Siblings, 3, 31–32, 57
Single parent, xxvi, xxvii, xxx
Siegel, Daniel J., 23
Skelos, Dean, xxiv
Skills, development of
    art. *See* Art, Painting, Drawing
    cognitive skills. *See* Cognitive development,
        Play, building cognitive skills
    computer skills, 9, 58, 115, 118, 137
    construction projects, 83

The Corwin Press logo—a raven striding across an open book—represents the union of courage and learning. Corwin Press is committed to improving education for all learners by publishing books and other professional development resources for those serving the field of PreK–12 education. By providing practical, hands-on materials, Corwin Press continues to carry out the promise of its motto: **"Helping Educators Do Their Work Better."**